Games, Ideas and Activities
for Primary Science

Other titles in the series

Games, Ideas
and **Activities** for
Primary Science

John Dabell

Longman
is an imprint of

Harlow, England • London • New York • Boston • San Francisco • Toronto
Sydney • Tokyo • Singapore • Hong Kong • Seoul • Taipei • New Delhi
Cape Town • Madrid • Mexico City • Amsterdam • Munich • Paris • Milan

Pearson Education Limited
Edinburgh Gate
Harlow CM20 2JE
United Kingdom
Tel: +44 (0)1279 623623
Fax: +44 (0)1279 431059
Website: www.pearsoned.co.uk

First edition published in Great Britain in 2010

© Pearson Education Limited 2010

The right of John Dabell to be identified as author of this work has been asserted
by him in accordance with the Copyright, Designs and Patents Act 1988.

Pearson Education is not responsible for the content of third party internet sites.

ISBN: 978-1-4082-2323-9

British Library Cataloguing in Publication Data
A CIP catalogue record for this book can be obtained from the British Library

Library of Congress Cataloging in Publication Data
Dabell, John.
   Games, ideas and activities for primary science / John Dabell.
      p. cm.
   Includes bibliographical references.
   ISBN 978–1–4082–2323–9 (pbk.)
  1. Science--Study and teaching (Primary)--Activity programs. I. Title.
   LB1585.D28 2010
   372.3'5--dc22

                     201002085

10 9 8 7 6 5 4 3 2
14 13 12

Set by 30 in 8.5/12pt NewsGothic BT
Printed by Ashford Colour Press Ltd., Gosport

Contents

Chapter 7
Science and literacy
activities

Appendices

This book is dedicated to Dr Matt Griffin and Dr Ian Sayers for their expertise and outstanding support.

Acknowledgements

We are grateful for permission to reproduce 'Warning' by Jenny Joseph, copyright © Jenny Joseph, *Selected Poems* (Bloodaxe, 1992). Reproduced with permission of Johnson & Alcock Ltd.

Introduction

The following poem is a scientific adaptation of the Jenny Joseph classic 'Warning'*

Warning - When I Am an Old Scientist

When I am an old scientist, I shall wear a tea cosy in the shape of a cottage.

With a hot water tank jacket which doesn't go and doesn't suit me.

And I shall spend my pension on rainbows and pinhole projectors

And horseshoe magnets and say we've no money for bicarbonate of soda

I shall sit down on a periscope when I am tired

And gobble up food chains in shops and press buzzers

And run my thermometer along endangered habitats

And make up for the surface tension of my youth.

I shall go out with my line graphs in the rain

And pick primary colours in other people's gardens

And learn to refract.

You can wear pendulums and grow more pigments

And eat three mini-beasts at a go

Or only micro-organisms for a week

And hoard shadows and femurs and echoes and things in boxes

But now we must have teaching techniques that make us obey

And pay our bills and not be inventive in class

And set a good example for the children.

We will have Ofsted inspectors to scrutinise and read the New Scientist

But maybe I ought to practise a little now?

* The full text of the original Jenny Joseph poem can be found in the appendices.

So people who know me are not too shocked and surprised

When suddenly I am old and start to wear a tea cosy in the shape of a cottage.

The science activities contained within this book put children and active learning first. The rationale is simple: to encourage children to think aloud in an atmosphere of respect for others' ideas.

You do not really understand something unless you can explain it to your grandmother. Albert Einstein

Where to start?

The book is organised into three main sections: Assessment, Curriculum and Creative Ideas.

In the first section there are two chapters in which you will find a variety of ideas for helping to assess children's comprehension of science concepts, ideas and processes. These contain clear strategies for finding out what children know and ideas for challenging them further.

In the second section of the book you will find a whole collection of experiments and investigations for trying out in class. These help to build children's knowledge, skills and understanding of life processes and living things, materials and their properties and physical processes.

In the third section of the book there are lots of creative ideas for hands-on and minds-on games, as well as a chapter devoted to bringing science to life through various literacy activities.

The chapters offer an exciting collection of 'talk-for-learning' ideas that can be used for starter activities, whole lesson and plenaries, or for use in science clubs or as homework challenges. The activities are intended to be accessible to all levels of ability, while appealing to a range of different learning styles and ages. Some require little or no preparation whereas others need some quality groundwork time.

The science gems in this book fulfil a range of purposes. You might use them as assessment for learning, reflection, making links and forward planning, or for presentation and celebration.

Have a look through and start with something you are interested in and adapt if necessary. When you know what it is you want to try, use the activity within a lesson and assess how effective it is as it develops.

Use the ideas here to build your own collection of science gems and share what works and what doesn't with your colleagues. The activities are not limited to science lessons – most can be used or modified to fit the needs of other lessons and subjects.

The 7Es

Many of the activities in this book can be used as part of a learning cycle called the 7Es. This is a way to help build learning based around children experiencing science for themselves before they are given a formal scientific explanation.

The 7Es breaks learning into 7 important components:

1. Engage

   The purpose of this stage is to hook children and get them interested and involved. Activities that children are given help them make connections between past and present learning experiences, and this helps set the scene for follow-on activities. Children are often presented with a Big Idea or Big Question in the context of a story or a strategy that provokes a lot of discussion.

2. Elicit

   The function of this stage is to find out what children know already, and any misconceptions they may hold. This tells you where you need to start from in building their understanding.

3. Explore

   In this stage children work together in groups, and build understanding based on first-hand experience. The teacher acts as a facilitator, providing materials and guiding the children's focus. The emphasis here is placed on questioning and critical thinking.

4. Explain

   In the explain stage children begin to communicate what they have learned. This happens between pairs, groups and the whole class, and gives everyone an opportunity to listen to alternative ideas and different ways of thinking. This is the time for a teacher to formalise learning with terminology, definitions, models and analogies.

5. Elaborate

   In this stage children deepen their understanding by applying what they now know to similar contexts. Children are given a range of contexts or problems to practise further so they can grasp the Big Idea.

6. Evaluate

   This is the assessment stage where everyone evaluates what they have learnt, what they are still unsure of and what they need to do next in order to build further understanding.

7. Extend

   In this stage children are challenged to transfer their learning to contexts quite different from the one they originally studied, apply their understanding to the world around them and make new connections.

This cycle is not a rigid formula, however, as you may decide to change the order, and even loop back to previous stages.

Companion website

For further ideas and support, access the companion website accompanying the book at **www.pearsoned.co.uk/dabell**, where you will find sections devoted to investigating, science puzzles, questions and prompts and group discussion.

Chapter 1
Assessment for learning ideas

'Mr Dabell, I think I've just had an Ulrika moment!'

'Do you mean a Eureka moment, Mitchell?'

Science lesson, summer term 2007

Introduction

The following activities are all starting points for science talk and so should be used to assess children's knowledge and understanding of science. Some could be used as starters, although many could be used as sandwich activities in the middle of a lesson. Some might develop into whole class lessons and others might be used as discrete challenges as part of a thinking skills session. All the activities are creative springboards for diving into pools of scientific learning, and are intended for children to splash about in.

You may also find the activities useful as 'brain-break activities' to make constructive use of time while children shift between one intensive activity and another, or when a disruption unsettles a class and they need to ease quickly back into productive work.

There are enough activities here to keep children on their toes, never knowing what you have up your sleeve from one lesson to the next. The danger of sticking to a few tried and tested activities is that they can quickly become part of a stagnant routine, resulting in activities that lack the essential sense of pace and challenge. To avoid these pitfalls, be mindful that activities need to be varied and active.

Alive or not alive

Alive or not alive challenges children to differentiate between living and non-living things.

Suitable for

KS1
KS2

Aim

- To help children understand that all living things grow, breathe, reproduce, excrete, respond to stimuli, and have similar basic needs such as nourishment.

Organisation

- This is suitable for small groups of two to four

Resources

- No special resources needed

What to do

- Write the following list of living and non-living things onto a piece of paper and photocopy:

  spider, silk, laptop, spoon, tree, jumper, slug, river, beetle, volcano, table, cake, knife, bottle, rock, icicle, DVD, elephant, earthworm, cotton, can, picture, buttercup, rain, calculator, snow, kettle, frog, clouds, fossil, milk, paper, leather, rubber, plastic.

- Ask children to look at the items on the list in pairs and talk about which they think are alive and which are not alive.
- Remind children that some of the things in the list could give the appearance of being alive but actually aren't.

- Ask children then to copy the names of the living and non-living things in the table below:

Alive	Not alive

- Children can now team up with another pair and discuss the following questions:
    1. What characteristics did all of the living things have in common?
    2. Did any of the non-living things possess some of the same characteristics as the living things? Which ones?
    3. How were the living things different from the non-living things?

Variations

- As a class, vote on each item in the list. Those characteristics not agreed upon will then be discussed. Encourage children to be open to the ideas of others and, at the same time, let someone know if they disagree, and why.
- You could present this activity using a Venn diagram.
- Another way to present the activity is shown below:

Item	Living thing	Non-living but once part of a living thing	Non-living and never part of a living thing
apple			
mushroom			
bathroom sponge			
sand			
woollen jumper			
light bulb			

Item	Living thing	Non-living but once part of a living thing	Non-living and never part of a living thing
paper bag			
coal			
rose			
automatic doors			
fire			
diamond			
olive oil			
cardboard			
petrol			

- Present a list of living and non-living things as a card-sort activity. For example:

bird	wool	fire	mud	rose	moss	car	wind
windmill	slug	cow	stone	cat	butterfly	egg	sheep
fish	tree	door	sunflower	coal	leather boots	rat	clock
milk	frog	grass	cloud	seaweed	ice	Moon	house

- After children have completed their tables, display them on the wall and discuss what different pairs have chosen as a whole class.

Challenge questions

- Can you think of your own list of living and non-living things?
- Can you write a definition of a living thing?
- If something is hibernating, then would you say that this is more like a non-living than a living thing?

Am I alive?

> Am I alive? encourages children to compare and contrast two things that appear similar in certain respects.

Suitable for

KS2

Aims

- To test children's knowledge of what makes a living thing.
- To identify common characteristics of living organisms.
- To define scientific classification.
- To explain how specific organisms are classified.
- To practise being sceptical and defending a position.

Organisation

This can be played as pairs, fours or as a whole class

Resources

- No special resources needed

What to do

- Begin the lesson by discussing living organisms. Ask children to tell you what separates a living thing from a non-living thing. Talk about the characteristics that living things share.
- Tell children that certain non-living things can be compared to living things and that they might appear to be the same in many ways.
- Ask children to think about how a helicopter and a bird might be similar to each other. Let children discuss this with a partner.

- Ask children to share their ideas with the rest of the class. Write down their ideas as they are given. Talk about whether a helicopter is alive if it can do some of the things a bird does. Stress the thinking process, and the backing up of opinions, rather than right or wrong answers.

- Write the comparisons as follows:

  Helicopter
  A helicopter has wings and flies in the sky.
  A seagull has wings and flies in the sky.
  A helicopter excretes waste.
  A seagull excretes waste.
  Is a helicopter alive?

- Talk about what makes something alive. What ideas can children think of?

- Try the activity again, this time thinking about another machine, such as a tank. Write about it compared to an elephant:

  Tank
  A tank is big and heavy and lumbers across the ground.
  An elephant is big and heavy and lumbers across the ground.
  A tank has a thick outer skin for protection.
  An elephant has a thick outer skin for protection.
  A tank burns fuel for energy.
  An elephant burns food for energy.
  A tank excretes waste.
  An elephant excretes waste.
  Is a tank alive?

- Children should work in teams to discuss the question: 'What do all living things have in common?' They should record their ideas and share their background knowledge. Then the groups should come together and try to reach consensus about the characteristics that all living things share by asking each other questions and defending their own ideas.

Variations

- Get children to invent their own 'Am I alive?' statements for a whale and a submarine, or something of their own choosing.
- Create a display of children's comparison verses.
- Have children look for examples of living and non-living things around the school.

Challenge questions

- Can you convince someone else that a cloud is a living thing because it moves and grows?
- What is the oldest living thing on Earth?
- What is the largest living thing on Earth?
- What is the smallest living thing on Earth?

Sequencing

Sequencing challenges children to place together various pictures into a logical sequence.

Suitable for

KS1

Aims

● To understand the importance of ordering events so that something makes sense.

Organisation

● Suitable for individuals and pairs

Resources

● Images from nature/science magazines
● Seeds
● Compost
● Plastic cups

What to do

● Talk about sequencing different parts of a story, such as the beginning, middle and end. Discuss why putting these parts into an order helps us understand.

● Now show children some pictures that have been mixed up: for example, the life cycle of a hen. Challenge children to place them in order from beginning to end to create a story.

● Children then write a description of the sequence underneath each picture.

Variations

- Have children hold the pictures to sequence in front of the class.
- Cut out sequences of events illustrated in a nature or science magazine: for example, the eruption of a volcano, the change of seasons, flowers to seeds, etc. For each set of illustrations, children can find a book that describes the event and put the illustrations in the correct sequence.
- Select random pictures from a magazine. Children can examine the pictures and put the pictures in an order that tells a story.
- Let children plant their own seeds in plastic cups. Put the planted seeds in a sunny spot in the room for observation. Take several sheets of white paper, fold them in half and staple them together to make observation journals. Children can draw a picture of what they see and label their pictures. These can then be used as a sequencing activity by mixing up the different stages of growth for children to order.

Challenge questions

- Can you draw some pictures of your own to show the life cycle of a frog or butterfly?
- Can you sequence something using a mixture of pictures and words?

Odd one out

Odd one out is an activity to help children recognise similarities and differences, and encourage them to see patterns and connections between objects and ideas.

Suitable for

KS1
KS2

Aims

- To compare and contrast objects, ideas, people and events.
- To express opinions and justify reasoning.
- To develop reasoning skills and knowledge.

Organisation

- This activity can be played as pairs, fours or as a whole class

Resources

- No special resources needed

What to do

- Choose a collection of objects or write down four words on the board: for example, car, bus, horse and plane.
- Ask children to work in pairs to choose which they think is the odd one out and why.
- Discuss ideas and listen to the reasons given. Explain that there is no right or wrong answer. Try to decide which reason is more convincing. For example, a horse might be the odd one out because it is the only living thing. A plane might be chosen because it is the only one that can fly.

- Repeat this activity again with a different list of four items, such as eagle, owl, bat, penguin. This time, children should play individually and write their answers on a whiteboard when prompted. Possible answers might include penguin because a penguin can't fly, bat because a bat has teeth and the others don't, or penguin because it is the only one living in the southern hemisphere.

- Now write the following lists on the board and ask children to select an odd one out from each row, giving a reason for their choice:

  1. castle, boat, key, shed
  2. table, television, teddy, chair
  3. cake, apple, pear, banana
  4. cow, sheep, pig, lion
  5. kangaroo, orange, kite, strawberry
  6. fish, shark, crocodile, monkey
  7. bat, bird, crab, plane

- Children could answer using a template like the one below to detail their thinking:

Why the shed could be the odd one out.	It is the only one made of wood.
Why the castle could be the odd one out.	It is the only one that is made of stone.
Why the boat could be the odd one out.	It is the only one that sells things.
Why the key could be the odd one out.	It is the only one that is made out metal.
We think that the odd one out from all the objects is the key because ...	It is used to open all the others.

Variations

- You might find that a clue helps if children are stumped. For example, which is the odd one out and why?

Bread
Yoghurt

Cereal

Cheese

Clue: which use microbes in their manufacture?

- Another format for doing an odd one out activity is to present a list inside a table for children to discuss row by row, but then mix it up and experiment by exchanging words from one list with another.

1	snail	slug	mussel	spider	octopus
2	water boatman	great diving beetle	tadpole	dragonfly	caddisfly
3	hyena	cheetah	lion	tiger	panther
4	bee	flea	wasp	dragonfly	butterfly
5	pelican	seagull	gannet	albatross	penguin
6	snake	frog	crocodile	alligator	lizard
7	starfish	crab	lobster	shrimp	woodlouse
8	caterpillar	maggot	worm	dragonfly larva	caddisfly larva
9	cow	sheep	horse	pig	chicken
10	whale	shark	dolphin	seal	porpoise

- Play the game for points. For example, if a unique reason can be found why an object is the odd one out then two points are scored.
- Children can develop their own sets in pairs (this could easily be set as a homework task).

Challenge questions

- Is it possible to have a true odd one out if you can think of a reason for each of the objects?
- Can you invent your own odd one out activity and think of two reasons why it might be the odd one out for every object you choose?
- Can you invent an odd one out activity for another topic?
- What skills do you use in this activity?

Diamond nine

Diamond nine involves discussing and prioritising nine objects, items or ideas, and justifying their position in a diamond pattern.

Suitable for

KS1
KS2

Aims

* To compare and contrast objects, ideas, people and events.
* To articulate thinking and support reasoning.
* To connect new ideas with what children know already.

Organisation

* This is best done as a pair or in a group of three

Resources

* Lists of statements such as the ones on page 15 made into cards or strips of paper

What to do

* Explain to children how a diamond nine activity works.
* Say that you are going to give them a collection of nine cards that they have to arrange into a diamond pattern by selecting:
* one card as the most important
  two cards as equal and next important
  three cards as those that are next most important
  two cards again that are less important
  one card that is least important

- The aim is to arrange nine alternatives in a diamond pattern like this:

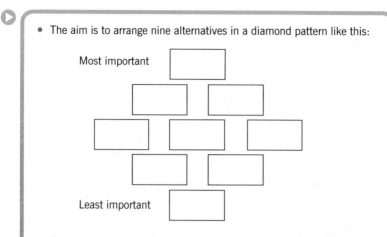

- Explain that eight cards have a statement on them but one has been left blank for them to complete.
- Now tell the children that you are going to ask them a question and they have to put the cards in order from most important to least important: for example, what is most important in being fit and keeping healthy?
  1. Drinking two litres of water a day.
  2. Taking a multi-vitamin tablet each day.
  3. Taking a nap in the afternoon.
  4. Exercising for about an hour per day.
  5. Exercising six hours a day for two days a week.
  6. Drinking two units of alcohol a day.
  7. Eating at least five portions of fruit or vegetables each day.
  8. Starting the day with a cooked breakfast.
  9. _____
- Children should then work together to try and agree what card should be placed where and why.
- After a period of 10–15 minutes, invite each group to present their top three priorities to the whole group and explain briefly why they chose them. What statement came bottom? Pick on any interesting or unusual feature of the priority order that particular groups have chosen in order to stimulate whole group reflection and discussion.
- Talk about the ninth card – what sort of statements did children select?

Variations

- You can write words or simple statements on Post-it notes rather than make cards.
- A diamond nine arrangement might not be suitable for all children. A diamond four might be better for some as it is a simpler format, whereas a diamond 12 would provide a higher level of challenge for more able learners. Using pictures on their own is one option or using a mixture of pictures and words is another way.
- Place the cards in a ladder rather than a diamond shape.
- Experiment with group size and include children of different abilities.

Challenge questions

- Can you make up another nine cards of your own, answering the same question above?
- Can you make a diamond nine activity for another group to try? For example, could you make diamond nine cards for materials to show how hard or soft they are?

Card sort

> Card sort challenges children to work collaboratively with others to match, sort or arrange a set of cards into specific groups or categories in a way that makes the most sense to them.

Suitable for

KS1
KS2

Aims

- To compare and contrast objects, ideas, people and events.
- To articulate thinking and support reasoning.
- To connect new ideas with what children know already.

Organisation

- This activity is best done as a pair or in a group of three

Resources

- Word lists cut into cards

What to do

- Cut out the cards below and divide children into small groups.

air	plasticine	sugar	stone	tomato sauce
paper	sand	metal	toothpaste	jelly
hot custard	concrete	nitrogen	water	pencil
cold custard	shaving cream	rubber	steam	foam

- Challenge children to sort the cards into three piles – one for solids, one for liquids and one for gases – and be ready to explain their decisions.
- When the cards have been sorted, ask different groups to list the contents of each of their piles, and justify their choices.

Variations

- You could sort some statements into 'true', 'false' or 'don't know' piles. For example:

> The North Pole is stronger than the South pole.
> Magnets only attract shiny objects.
> You can destroy a magnet by freezing it.
> It is dangerous to touch some magnets.
> Magnets become weaker if you don't use them.
> Only the pole of a magnet attracts.
> You can make a nail into a magnet.
> Marble magnets are stronger than ring magnets.
> Magnets are made of aluminium and copper.
> If you cut a magnet in half it makes a new magnet.
> A compass always points south.

- By making the cards slightly larger, you can add some simple questions.
- Include blank cards for children to write their own ideas.
- Number cards so that missing ones can easily be identified and replaced.
- Use different colours for the cards.

Challenge questions

- How useful was the card sort in making you think?
- How could you improve a card sort?
- What other topics in science could you use a card sort for?

Auction site advert

Auction site advert brings science to life in a familiar and fun context by challenging children to create their own version of an online auction advert.

Suitable for

KS1
KS2

Aims

- To help children spot deliberate mistakes in a text and diagram.
- To help improve subject knowledge and understanding.

Organisation

- An activity for pairs or threes

Resources

- Auction site examples/template

What to do

- Explain to children that the idea of this activity is to select a science object you wish to sell, describe it, fix a price and place an advert for it in the style of an online auction site.

- Look at some carefully chosen examples of real-life auction sites to familiarise children with their style and content.

- Show an example you have created and point out that your advert deliberately contains some mistakes that they have to spot. Explain that many online auction descriptions do contain errors and so this teaches children to read for accuracy and reliability.

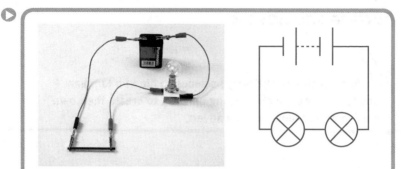

If you're looking for a series circuit then this could be the one for you! This well constructed closed circuit is made up of one bulb, two batteries, wires and a breadboard. This would make an ideal gift for anyone thinking about setting up a Christmas tree display. Comes with its own circuit diagram for you to follow. Happy bidding!

- Ask children to talk in pairs and discuss what they think might be wrong with the advert and circuit diagram.
- Take feedback from everyone and have a go at rewriting the advert so that it is accurate.
- Now challenge children to create their own auction site advert.

Variations

- Provide a partially completed advert for children to correct and complete.
- Design a science poster containing deliberate mistakes to sell online.
- Write a letter of complaint about the advert, stating what you think is wrong with it.
- Adapt this activity so that children sell something scientific in the style of a presenter on a shopping channel.

Challenge questions

- Can you create some auction adverts for a science competition?
- Can you create an erroneous advert for another group to correct?

That's strange!

That's strange! involves searching for something unusual to capture children's attention and gives everyone something to ponder and discuss.

Suitable for

KS1
KS2

Aims

- To help children question and discuss the world around them.
- To use observations, measurements or other data to draw conclusions.

Organisation

- An activity for pairs or threes

Resources

- No special resources needed

What to do

- Ask children to imagine that they went shopping at their local supermarket and they noticed it had started selling pink milk. Ask children to think of ideas as to what turned the milk pink and whether they would buy it. Give some examples such as:

    It has turned pink because someone has added a food colouring.
    It has turned pink because the cow has eaten beetroot.
    It has turned pink because the cow was bleeding.

- What questions would children ask about the pink milk? Examples might include:

    Is pink milk safe?
    What does it taste like?
    Is it healthier than white milk?

- Before telling the children that cows have actually produced pink milk, ask them what colour a carrot is. Most children will say orange without hesitation but that isn't the only possible colour. Explain that pink milk is actually caused by cows eating orange carrots combined with their diet of grass and hay. It has been found that feeding cows white carrots turns the milk white again. Ask children: what other colours can a carrot be? Why do we mostly see orange carrots?

Variations

- This activity could be turned into a concept cartoon-style discussion. Write on the board the following opinions and see what children think about them:

    1. White milk is better for you because it contains more nutrients.
    2. The pink milk has been contaminated so you shouldn't drink it.
    3. Both pink and white milk will be good for you.

- Can children think of their own concept cartoon conversations?
- To inspire children's thinking in a similar way, try to think of other interesting or unusual situations where there is a simple and scientific explanation to hand.

Challenge questions

- What colour are corn-fed chickens?
- Would we change colour if we ate just one colour of food? Would our urine be the colour of the food?

Rumours

> Rumours presents children with scientific rumours as a useful way of developing discussions based on misconceptions. These rumours can be shared and investigations planned around them.

Suitable for

KS1
KS2

Aims

- To generate ideas by drawing on their own and other people's experiences.
- To develop ideas and explain them clearly.

Organisation

- An activity for pairs or threes

Resources

- No special resources needed

What to do

- Talk about the word 'rumour' and what it means.
- Tell children that you have some scientific rumours that you need their help in investigating.
- Start with the following rumour and ask children to think about whether they agree or disagree: 'I heard a rumour that when teeth fall out new ones grow back.'
- Ask children to talk about the rumour in pairs and decide whether it refers to human teeth or not.

- Discuss as a class whether all animals have teeth that grow back. For example, when rodents use up their teeth, other teeth replace them immediately. Sharks have thousands of teeth in their lifetime. A tiger shark sheds more than 2,000 teeth every year. A follow-on from this activity would be to ask children to choose an animal and research books and the internet to find out:

  Where does your animal live? What is its habitat?
  How many teeth does the animal have?
  What does your animal eat? Is your animal a herbivore, a carnivore, or an omnivore?
  How are your animal's teeth adapted to getting and eating its food?

- Select other rumours for children to investigate. Select from the following or create your own:

  ... if you put a magnet in a freezer it will destroy it.
  ... electricity gets used up when it goes round a circuit.
  ... rain comes from holes in clouds.
  ... plastic is attracted to a magnet.
  ... all plants have seeds.
  ... batteries have electricity inside them.
  ... water doesn't evaporate on a cloudy day.
  ... all metals are magnetic.
  ... the roots of plants are green.
  ... all objects containing air float.
  ... some black objects are translucent.
  ... a gas doesn't weigh anything.
  ... sound travels more quickly in liquids than in solids.
  ... loud sounds can make you deaf.
  ... big instruments make louder noises than small ones.
  ... car tyres protect you from lightning.
  ... a shadow is longer at night.
  ... light travels further at night than in daytime.
  ... heat rises.
  ... mirrors reverse everything.
  ... some seeds can lay dormant for over 1,000 years.
  ... hitting an object harder changes its pitch.
  ... there is more carbon dioxide in the air at night.

... a push is bigger than a pull.

... a seed needs sunlight to grow.

... a puddle will evaporate quicker in the afternoon.

Variation

- You can choose to theme rumours. Here are some rumours based on Earth and the Moon. I heard a rumour that ...

    ... the Moon is a star.

    ... the Sun disappears at night.

    ... the Sun moves across the sky during the day.

    ... the amount of daylight increases each day of summer.

    ... gravity is stronger on the equator.

    ... water goes down plugholes anti-clockwise in the southern hemisphere.

    ... the Sun orbits the Earth.

    ... there is a dark side of the Moon.

    ... the phases of the moon are caused by a shadow from the Earth.

    ... a solar eclipse occurs when the Sun passes between the Moon and the Earth.

    ... the Moon has no gravity.

    ... there is no gravity in space.

    ... planets a long way from the Sun have less gravity or no gravity.

    ... there is no gravity in space.

    ... gravity doesn't just act as a downwards force.

    ... you can turn gravity on and off.

    ... gravity is stronger on the ground.

    ... gravity increases with height.

    ... gravity requires a medium to act through.

Challenge questions

- Can you create your own science rumours for another pair to investigate?
- Can you write some science rumours for another school to answer?

That's because

> That's because involves children thinking of a hypothetical situation for others to try to problem solve.

Suitable for

KS1
KS2

Aims

- To generate ideas by drawing on their own and other people's experiences.
- To talk about what information they need and how they can find and use it.
- To develop and refine ideas collaboratively.

Organisation

- An activity for pairs or threes

Resources

- No special resources needed

What to do

- Tell children that you have made a circuit but that you need help to understand why it doesn't work. Write this on the board: 'My circuit doesn't work ...'
- Ask children to volunteer their ideas about what might be wrong. Explain that you'd like the answer to be given using the following words: 'That's because ...' followed by their reason. Responses have to be different. Some possible responses are as follows:

    'That's because your battery is dead.'
    'That's because the wires inside the plastic are broken.'
    'That's because there is a break in the connection.'

'That's because the filament has burnt away.'
'That's because there isn't an electrical current.'
'That's because there aren't enough batteries.'
'That's because the bulb isn't screwed in.'
'That's because you only have one wire.'

- As each reason is volunteered you can write it down on a whiteboard and discuss them in more detail later.
- Show children the circuit you have made and share with them the actual reason or reasons why it isn't working.
- Now think of another scenario to get children thinking. For example, 'My plant won't grow ...'

Variations

- Working in pairs, children can think of their own scientific situations for the rest of the class to problem solve.
- Set some scenarios as homework for children to complete.

Challenge questions

- Can you think of a real-life science situation at home that you could problem solve? For example, 'My bike has a flat tyre ...'
- Can you think of the situation given the solutions? Write down two or three solutions to a problem for someone else to guess the situation they might be trying to answer.

My mistake

My mistake involves describing how to do an experiment, drawing a diagram, explaining an idea or writing something on the whiteboard, but with a mistake or mistakes for children to spot.

Suitable for

KS1
KS2

Aims

- To question and make thoughtful observations about scientific concepts, ideas and statements.
- To identify and explain different views that people hold about scientific ideas.

Organisation

- An activity for pairs or threes

Resources

- Statements or images that include deliberate mistakes

What to do

- Children work in pairs to spot the error or errors contained in a statement and share their thoughts with other pairs.
- As a whole class, the mistakes are discussed and corrected.
- For example, look at the following statements and decide what the mistakes are:

A clinometer is a device used for measuring forces.

An amphibian is covered with hair and feeds milk to its babies.

Sharp teeth that are good for tearing food are called molars.

A microscope is any living thing that is too small to be seen with the naked eye.

Materials that come from the earth and can be used by living things are called artificial resources: for example, water, oil, and minerals.

During the last big winter storm, condensation took the form of snow and sleet.

- Discuss the mistakes and write the statements out again accurately.

Variations

- Use a picture and ask children to circle the mistakes they can see. For example:

In this example there are no arrowheads indicated. These would need to be drawn on to illustrate the direction of travel from the light source, reflecting from the cat and into the person's eyes.

- My mistake could be extended to a game of 'Spot the difference' in which children are shown two pictures with one showing a mistake or mistakes.
- Use this strategy and present information inside a table. For example:

	North Pole of a bar magnet	South Pole of a bar magnet
Steel paperclip	attracts	repels
North Pole of a horseshoe magnet	repels	attracts
South Pole of a rod magnet	repels	repels
10p piece	does not attract	attracts

Challenge questions

- Can you describe an experiment to the rest of your table or class that contains a deliberate mistake?
- Can you draw your own scientific diagram that shows an idea but contains a mistake for another group to spot?

If ... then

If ... then is a fun matching activity and an excellent way of joining ideas together.

Suitable for

KS1
KS2

Aims

- To investigate a concept and make decisions about its validity.
- To explain reasoning when problem solving.
- To use scientific communication and explanation skills.

Organisation

- An activity for pairs or threes

Resources

- Mixed-up 'if ... then' cards

What to do

- Give children a list of mixed-up 'if ... then' pairs of cards to cut up.
- Children then discuss the ideas in pairs and match the 'if' to the correct 'then'.

If	Then
You change one thing in an experiment ...	... it will fall back down to earth.
You eat too much sugar ...	... it has a domino effect.
You don't water a plant ...	... you may become ill.
You throw a ball into the air ...	... they make an emulsion and eventually separate.
You run around for five minutes ...	... it's a fair test.
You don't wash your hands frequently ...	... you may get tooth decay and put on weight.
You change something in a food chain ...	... it will wilt and die.
You whisk oil and water ...	... it sticks to the surface.
You rub a balloon on a jumper and hold it against a wall or ceiling ...	... your reflection is upside down.
You look at yourself in the back of a spoon	... your heart will beat faster.

- Discuss which 'If' cards were the hardest to match up.
- Talk about the correct matches and discuss whether they could be improved.

Variations

- You could do this activity in the style of a more conventional matching exercise which poses a question and then encourages children to link the answer.
- Cut out the table into cards and give individual children a question or answer card. Children have to find whom they match up with.

What kind of covering does an amphibian have?	Moist skin
What kind of covering does a reptile have?	Dry scales
What kind of covering does a bird have?	Feathers
What kind of covering does a mammal have?	Hair or fur
What kind of covering does a fish have?	Wet scales
Which vertebrate groups lay eggs in water?	Amphibians and fish
Which vertebrate group gives birth to live young?	Mammals
Which group of vertebrates lays jelly-coated eggs?	Amphibians
Which group of vertebrates lays eggs with hard shells?	Birds
Which group of vertebrates lays eggs with leathery shells?	Reptiles
What feature do all vertebrates have in common?	A backbone
How many legs do insects have?	Six
How do plants make their own food?	By photosynthesis

Challenge questions

- Can you invent a matching exercise where a question might have more than one correct answer?
- Can you invent your own matching exercise for the school's website?

Always–sometimes–never–not sure

Always – sometimes – never – not sure is a discussion-rich exercise for testing the validity of various scientific statements. It is frequently referred to as a true–false exercise, but having two extra categories (sometimes and not sure) means there is more opportunity for a richer discussion.

Suitable for

KS1
KS2

Aims

* To investigate a statement and make decisions about its validity.
* To use scientific communication and explanation skills.

Organisation

* An activity for pairs or threes

Resources

* No special resources needed

What to do

* Tell children that you have collected together some statements from different magazines that you'd like them to discuss together. Ask children to make four headings on a piece of paper:

    Always   Sometimes   Never   Not Sure

* Explain that each statement needs to be placed under one of the four headings. Write the following statements on the board and let children discuss them:

1. Crisps are high in fat.
2. Chips are bad for you.
3. Food cooked at home is better for you than ready meals.
4. Carbohydrates give you energy.
5. Protein gives you muscles.
6. All foods make you grow.
7. Salt is bad for you.

- After some discussion time, children can share their placements and explain their reasoning to the rest of the class.
- Talk about which statements were the most clear-cut and which the most contentious.
- Try to reach agreement about where the statements should be placed.
- Now look at another set of statements and discuss those. For example:

1. Solids can flow.
2. The particles in solids are held together with strong bonds.
3. Solids are difficult to squash.
4. There are spaces between the particles in a solid.
5. Liquids are easy to squash.
6. The particles in a liquid are a long way apart.
7. Liquids can change shape.
8. Particles in a liquid are close together.

- The statements can be displayed or read out to pupils to respond to either on paper or on mini-whiteboards.
- You may find that just one statement on its own may well be sufficient to promote fruitful discussion.

Variation

- The activity could be run as a trial, with groups of children giving their evidence and the rest of the class (the jury) deciding if it proves or disproves the statement. This could be very useful if different groups have worked on different statements and you need their work to be shared with the whole class.

Challenge question

* Can you invent your own statements for another class to discuss? These can be mixed or themed. For example:

1. Your mass would be the same on the Earth and on the Moon.
2. The Earth has a stronger force of gravity than the Moon.
3. Your weight would be less on the Earth than on the Moon.
4. The Earth has a stronger force of gravity than the Moon.
5. Your body will sink in water.
6. The upthrust from the water balances your weight.
7. A lump of iron will float in water.
8. The upthrust from the water balances its weight.

1. Friction always slows things down.
2. Vehicles need friction to keep moving.
3. You could not move without friction.
4. Friction is useful to a waiter.
5. Shoelaces stay tied up because of friction.
6. You could not pick up a cup of tea without friction.
7. You could drink from a glass without friction.
8. Snow increases the friction between your shoes and the ground.
9. Friction is useful in playgrounds.
10. There is no friction when you are ice skating.

1. Food chains always start with a plant.
2. Herbivores only eat plants.
3. Herbivores and carnivores are producers.
4. Herbivores and carnivores eat other organisms.
5. Predators are always carnivores.
6. A predator is an animal that only eats plants.
7. You need to use a food web to show the feeding relationships in a habitat.
8. Most animals eat only one type of plant or animal.
9. Plants can't eat animals.

1. You see light as soon as a light bulb is switched on.
2. Light does not take any time to travel from the bulb to your eyes.
3. Transparent objects cause shadows.
4. The sun's energy is inside all of us.
5. Light cannot travel through opaque objects.

6. Luminous objects are sources of light.
7. We see non-luminous objects because they absorb light.
8. Light travels in straight lines.
9. Light can go through transparent materials.

Concept cartoons

Concept cartoons uses cartoon-style conflict discussion boards or visual disagreements to promote scientific conversations. The viewpoints presented are all different and it is this difference that acts as a catalyst for further conversations as learners talk together to discuss their thinking.

Suitable for

KS1
KS2

Aims

* To investigate a statement and make decisions about its validity.
* To use scientific communication and explanation skills.

Organisation

* An activity for pairs or threes

Resources

* Examples of concept cartoons

What to do

* Show children an example of a concept cartoon and explain what one is. See www.scienceonthesubway.com/cartoon-moonlight.html
* Explain that it is their job to join in the conversation and offer their opinions. For example:

    The horseshoe magnet is the strongest because it has two ends.
    A ring magnet is stronger because it attracts in every direction.

A disc magnet will be the strongest because it doesn't have a hole in the middle.

The biggest will always be the strongest.

- Allow children to reflect individually on the challenge before working together.
- Now encourage small group discussion to allow children to share ideas.
- Provide opportunities for feedback across the class about the alternatives partway through discussions.
- Play devil's advocate and challenge children's viewpoints and statements.
- Talk about what investigation could be planned to help understand the problem further.
- Plan an investigation and carry it out to help inform the conversation.
- Share results and ideas.
- Look at other concept cartoons together. For example:

Dogs and cats burn more calories than we do.
Dogs and cats don't have to watch their weight like us.
Dogs and cats can eat what they want.
They will put on weight if they don't eat the right foods.

I think tissue paper will soak up the mess.
Cardboard will soak up more because it's thicker.
A kitchen towel will work the best because it has layers.
What about using a sponge?

Variations

- Speech bubble ideas can be written on whiteboards for children to hold in front of the class.
- Have a concept cartoon competition to see who can create the most imaginative conversation.
- Use the cartoons for a science club activity.
- Use the cartoons as part of a science fair or open evening to stimulate talk.

Challenge question

- Can you create your own concept cartoons and present them with one correct speech bubble and the other three incorrect, or two correct answers and two incorrect, or with all answers being correct?

Review diagrams

Review diagrams challenges children to draw and annotate a picture as a way of assessing their thinking about a key concept.

Suitable for

KS1
KS2

Aims

- To assess knowledge and understanding of key concepts.
- To build on prior knowledge through the sharing of ideas.

Organisation

- An activity for pairs or threes

Resources

- No special resources needed

What to do

- Ask children to draw a picture of the world with four rain clouds around it, one on top, one on the bottom and one either side. Stress that this should be done without talking to anyone.
- After a short time, ask children to show you what they have drawn.
- If the drawings have been done on paper, collect them together and display them for everyone to see.
- Now talk through some of the drawings as a class, asking for comments and opinions about what has been drawn.

- Have they drawn the rain falling to Earth or away from Earth? Talk about why rain in the southern hemisphere does not fall into space. Imagine a game of cricket in South Africa – when a batsman hits the ball up into the air, does it reach the sky and go into space? Discuss the different sketches to help develop the notion of gravity acting towards the centre of the Earth. Share a scientific explanation of gravity and give children the opportunity of drawing the rain clouds a second time if they want to.

Variations

- A variation of this activity is to show children a picture Google Earth and use an application such as that from www.wizteach.com so that you can draw a picture of a person dropping a stone in the northern hemisphere compared to someone dropping a stone in the southern hemisphere.
- Weblink with a school in the southern hemisphere and ask them to do the same experiment as you. Compare their results with yours.
- Have children sit back to back, each with a whiteboard and pen. One child is given a picture of something to describe. For example, child A describes a picture of a circuit diagram which child B has to replicate. The drawings are compared and child B then describes a new visual for child A to complete.
- Ask children to close their eyes. Tell them that they are going to draw a picture using their mind's eye following your instructions. For example: 'Imagine you have a whiteboard and pen. We'll call the whiteboard your page. Write your name in the top right-hand corner. Draw a horizontal line in the middle of your page and draw a cat sitting on the line. Now draw the Sun in the top left-hand corner of your page. I want you to draw the cat's shadow. What does it look like? Where will you draw it?' Now ask children to open their eyes and give them a real whiteboard and pen to draw what they imagined. Compare and contrast by sharing their pictures together.
- Children close their eyes. Read part of a short story, passage, explanation or investigation to the class. Tell them to imagine what is happening in their mind. When you have finished reading, tell children to keep their eyes closed and continue to 'run the movie' in their minds for one minute. Take feedback from class about what happened in their mind movies. Can they draw what they have seen?

Challenge question

- Can you draw a poster to illustrate a scientific concept or process?

Word definitions

> Word definitions challenges children to write down what they think a concept means, revealing what they know, partly know and don't know about a key idea.

Suitable for

KS1
KS2

Aims

- To assess prior knowledge and understanding of key concepts.
- To build on prior knowledge through the sharing of ideas.

Organisation

- An activity for pairs or threes

Resources

- No special resources needed

What to do

- Show children the following words and ask them to think about which ones they have heard of before and what they mean:

    block, light, mirror, image, reflect, source, object, shadow, translucent, transparent, opaque

Challenge questions

- Can you collect dictionary definitions of words and use them to write your own definition?
- Can you write a word definition for a particular age group?

- Ask them to complete the table as shown below:

Words I know	Words I know a little about	Words I don't know
block	reflect	translucent
light	transparent	opaque
mirror		
image		
source		
object		
shadow		

- Children then work in groups to write down their own corporate definition of the words they know.

Words I know	Our definition
shadow	A reflection of something that you can't see through.
block	Something that stops light passing through.
light	Rays from the sun.
source	Something you put on your food.

- The definitions that teams of children give can then be shared with the whole class or another team and definitions refined, improved and polished.
- Any new words and/or definitions met in a lesson could be written on a piece of card and put into a shoebox. The words can then be picked out at any point for different pupils to explain what they mean.

Variations

- Another way to present word definitions is to adapt a KWL grid so that it looks like this:

Words I KNOW already	Words I WANT to know more about	Words that I have LEARNED today
shadow light mirror	block source object image	

- Share 'faulty' definitions with the class which you have created from fictitious pupils. Can they correct them?

Chapter 2
Graphic organisers

'Clouds are high flying fogs.'

Introduction

We live in a highly visual world, so using graphic organisers (GO) to help structure learning makes a lot of sense. A graphic organiser or cognitive organiser is a visual and graphic display that depicts the relationships between facts and ideas. These tools allow children to make their thinking visible and make sense of complex content by exploring and visually representing linkages and relationships.

Graphic organisers can help children understand information much more easily and they are often less intimidating than a piece of text. They help children to search for patterns and they provide an organised tool for making conceptual connections. They are effective tools for creative thinking as they help children to:

- Represent abstract ideas in more concrete forms.
- Depict the relationships among facts and concepts.
- Store and recall information.
- Clarify relationships, organise thoughts, and formulate ideas.
- Question and discover.

In this chapter you will find a collection of graphic organisers to help children think, plan and write. They come in all shapes and sizes, and use grids, tables, charts, lines, circles, symbols and other visual elements to show comparisons, contrasts, parts of a whole, classifications and other relationships. Graphic organisers can be used and adapted within any topic area, and of course, across the curriculum.

Graphic organisers can be used before a lesson as springboards for learning to activate prior knowledge, guide thinking, and develop vocabulary. You might want to use them during a lesson to help children organise information and stay focused on the content material, or after a lesson to confirm or rethink prior knowledge and to relate the new concepts to the old. They can also be used for challenges or for homework. There are different ways to use them. Sometimes you might choose to give children a blank graphic organiser and ask them to complete it from scratch. This can work but it can be daunting for some learners. A more productive way of using them is to provide a partially completed graphic that children add to. There are a couple of ways of doing this. You could provide completely accurate information or have a graphic organiser that contains some deliberate mistakes. This is down to you and your judgement of what will work best for your children, but graphic organisers that contain inaccuracies certainly get tongues wagging a whole lot more. The examples in this chapter show some graphic organisers that contain accurate information and some with mistakes but all are incomplete. The graphic organisers can be used independently but are best used for paired or small group thinking and discussion.

A to Z brainstorm

A to Z brainstorm is useful for listing the range of vocabulary associated with a topic and can be used at the beginning of a series of lessons or at the end. Not all of the boxes need to be filled in – some grids might contain a lot of words, some only a few.

Suitable for

KS1
KS2

Aims

* To build on each other's contributions and chain them together into coherent lines of thinking.
* To build on previous knowledge and create new understanding.
* To share information and solve problems together.

Organisation

* This is suitable for small groups of two to four

Resources

* A to Z template

What to do

* Show children a version of the A to Z grid below on the interactive whiteboard and explain that you want children to fill in the grid with as many topic words as they can think of.
* Ask for a few examples to get the grid started.

- Point out that they don't have to fill in every box. Stress that some boxes will have more than one word.

- As children start to think, one word leads to another and the grid starts to fill up pretty quickly.

- After an agreed deadline, stop and share to see what sorts of words have been used.

- Continue for a few more minutes and then let children swap their grid with one another to compare and contrast ideas.

Ourselves

A arm	G	M	S see, sight, sense, smell
B body, beak	H hearing, human	N nose	T touch
C	I	O	U
D	J	P	V
E ear	K	Q	W wing
F feel	L	R	X, Y, Z

Variations

- Provide children with science dictionaries, books and access to the internet so they can search for more words.
- Certain groups can search for particular letters to make the task less onerous.
- Offer points to the groups who can fill in the most boxes.
- For any letters that children can't fill in, they can invent some science words of their own with definitions to match.

Challenge questions

- Can you write dictionary definitions for the words that you have found?
- Can you collect as many words as possible during a topic and turn it into a personal wordwall?
- Can you write a science story with the words you have in your A–Z grid?

KWHL

> KWHL grids are excellent thinking tools that are used at the beginning and end of a topic. When beginning a unit of work a KWHL grid will help children to identify what they know about the topic, see what gaps there are in their knowledge, organise their thinking about what they need to do to find out more and reflect on what they have learnt and how they can apply it to new situations.

Suitable for

KS1
KS2

Aims

- To build on each other's contributions and chain them together into coherent lines of thinking.
- To build on previous knowledge and create new understanding.
- To share information and solve problems together.

Organisation

- This is suitable for small groups of two to four

Resources

- KWHL template

What to do

- Show children a blank KWHL grid and explain what each of the letters stands for.
- Look at the partially completed KWHL grid below and ask children to think of anything they disagree with or don't understand. Point out that

mistakes may have been made and it is their job to decide whether the information is accurate or not.

- Can they help to complete the grid? Ask children why the last part of the grid hasn't been filled in.

K	W	H	L
What we know about teeth.	We wonder ... What we want to know?	How will we find out more?	What have we learnt?
They fall out and new ones grow every year.	Why do they fall out? Where do they go?	Search the web.	
We have different types of teeth.	What types are there? What are they made of?	Books from school library.	
We have to clean them.	What can I use to clean them apart from toothpaste?	Search the web.	
The dentist looks after them.	Why must we visit a dentist regularly?	Ask a dentist to come and talk to us.	

- Based on your current topic, now give children a blank KWHL grid to complete, or a partially completed one that you have already started.
- When children have completed what they can, share ideas under each heading and give children opportunities to challenge each other.
- Explain that the last column of the grid can only be completed at the end of the topic.

- Think about how you could use KWHL grids in another topic: for example, grouping objects, materials, plants, living things and non-living things, being healthy, senses, sound, heat and light, Earth and the Moon, and so on.

Variations

- Show children completed KWHL grids from previous lessons and year groups to compare and contrast learning.
- Let children swap their grids with each other to peer assess and comment on each other's work.
- Ask children to invent their own KWHL grid with some deliberate mistakes for another group to discuss.

Challenge questions

- Is it possible to answer all the questions in a KWHL grid?
- Can you adapt the KWHL grid to further support learners to create their own questions and lines of thinking? For example:

What do I know?	What do I want to know?	What questions will I ask?	How will these questions help me to find out what I want to know?

Think-pair-share

Think–pair–share pairs up children to think, discuss and formulate a joint answer to a question using a think–share grid.

Suitable for

KS1
KS2

Aims

- To build on each other's contributions and chain them together into coherent lines of thinking.
- To build on previous knowledge and create new understanding.
- To share information and solve problems together.

Organisation

- This is suitable for small groups of two to four

Resources

- Think–share template

What to do

- Ask children to think about the following question: 'Do plants need water to grow?' Ask for answers to the question beyond just a straight 'yes' or 'no'.
- Now ask children to team up with a friend and share ideas. Do they agree with each other?
- Give children the think–share grid on page 56 and get them to complete each section. They will need to combine their answers to complete the last column.

- Challenge children to think of more questions they could ask and answer those too.
- Share ideas as a whole class to build thinking and understanding further.

Growing plants

Question	What I think	What my partner thinks	What we will share
Do plants need water to grow?	I think plants can grow with certain types of water: for example, unpolluted.	My partner thinks that plants can grow if you give them tea.	We think that plants can grow so long as they have a fluid which is clean.
Does a plant need light to grow?	I think plants will die without light.	My partner says that her plants at home are fine in the morning so don't need light to grow.	We think plants can grow in light and at night.

Variations

- Give children a completed think–share grid to discuss and improve.
- Test some of the answers given to check their validity: for example, feed a plant cola for a week to see if the plant grows.
- Create another column to formulate a 'class response' after group discussions have been shared.

Challenge questions

- Can you create a think–share grid of your own that contains deliberate mistakes for another group to find?
- Can you adapt the grid to include another category? For example: what resources will help us find out more?

Logical reasoning

In this activity children find similarities and distinctions between two or more things with the aim of answering a question or to find out more about a topic or concept.

Suitable for

KS1
KS2

Aims

- To build on each other's contributions and chain them together into coherent lines of thinking.
- To build on previous knowledge and create new understanding.
- To share information and solve problems together.

Organisation

- This is suitable for small groups of two to four

Resources

- Logical reasoning grid

What to do

- Ask children to think about the following question: 'Is an apple more like an orange than a banana?'
- Ask children to formulate an answer ready to share with the class.
- Most children will jump to say that an apple is more like an orange but, using a logical reasoning grid, this might not be so black and white!
- Show children the partially completed grid on page 58 and challenge them to complete the rest and question any mistakes they think have been made.

Health and growth

	Apple	Orange	Banana
shape	round		
edible seeds		no	
edible skin			yes
citrus family	yes		
peelable with a knife		no	
colour when ripe			green

- When children have completed the grid, ask the original question again and see whether children want to revise their original answer.
- Explain to children that the answer to the question depends entirely upon which set of criteria is used.

Variations

- Try this activity again using pear, watermelon and kiwi fruit, or strawberry, raspberry and blueberry.
- You could compare and contrast more than three items to make the activity more demanding.

Challenge questions

- Can you think of some questions you would ask a scientist based on your completed grid?
- How might your grid be used to solve a science problem in the real world?

Compare and contrast

Compare and contrast grids place two ideas, objects or things side by side and invite children to think about what ways they are the same and what ways they aren't.

Suitable for

KS1
KS2

Aims

- To build on each other's contributions and chain them together into coherent lines of thinking.
- To build on previous knowledge and create new understanding.
- To share information and solve problems together.

Organisation

- This is suitable for small groups of two to four

Resources

- Compare and contrast grid

What to do

- Ask children to think of ways in which bees and wasps are the same. Take ideas from the class.
- Now ask children to think of ways in which they are different. Share ideas again.
- Explain to children that one way of comparing and contrasting two things like this is to use a grid as a way of helping their thinking.

- Show children the grid below on your interactive whiteboard and talk about the comparisons made. Discuss the boxes that have been completed so far. Do they agree with them?

- Give children time to think through their own answers and see if they can complete the table. There are some blank boxes for them to add their own comparison criteria.

- After children have had time to complete their tables as far as they can, discuss as a class the similarities and differences.

- As you go through the table it will be obvious that upon closer examination a honeybee and a wasp show quite a lot of differences.

Honeybee	Comparison	Wasp
rounded	**body shape**	slender and smooth
pollen and nectar	**food**	
	legs	round and waxy with few hairs
honeybee dies after stinging	**sting**	
	nests	
	wings	two
	aggressiveness	
	hives	

- Here is another compare and contrast grid for plants and animals. This one has been completed for the categories given but children may be able to think of more ideas.

Plants	Comparison	Animals
stay in one place or get moved by wind, water or animals	**movement**	can move around by themselves
give off oxygen and take in carbon dioxide	**breathing**	take in oxygen and give off carbon dioxide
make food from sunlight, carbon dioxide, water and minerals	**food**	eat plants and other animals
produce seeds which grow into new plants	**giving birth**	lay eggs, which hatch later, or give birth to live young

Variations

- Other things to consider feeding into a compare and contrast grid include: a turtle and a tortoise; a vegetable and a fruit; a living plant and an artificial plant; the roots of a plant and the roots of a seedling; a stalactite and an icicle; and so on.
- When looking at one thing in particular – for example, seeds – it may be useful to compare and contrast using a simple matrix such as the following partially completed one:

Name of seed	Picture	Colour	Length
apple		dark brown	6 mm
pumpkin		light tan	15 mm
sunflower			
tomato			
banana			
peach			
potato			

- Another way to present compare and contrast grids is to look at more than one pair at a time. For example:

	Similarity	Difference
spider and insect	they are both found in the house	the spider has eight legs, the insect has six legs
amphibian and reptile		
bird and bat		
killer whale and shark		
snake and eel		
millipede and centipede		
octopus and jellyfish		
slug and worm		
duck and frog		
penguin and seal		

Challenge questions

- Can you design a science poster using the information in your compare and contrast grid?
- Can you compile a science report about the similarities and differences you have found?

Venn diagrams

In this activity, children use a sorting diagram to differentiate between information and appreciate their similarities. Venn diagrams are excellent tools for making features and characteristics more obvious, and they help children to articulate their thinking more clearly.

Suitable for

KS1
KS2

Aims

- To build on each other's contributions and chain them together into coherent lines of thinking.
- To build on previous knowledge and create new understanding.
- To share information and solve problems together.

Organisation

- This is suitable for small groups of two to four

Resources

- Venn diagram templates
- PE hoops
- Strips of paper

What to do

- Place two different-coloured PE hoops on the floor and label one 'Whale' and the other 'Dolphin'.
- Give children some strips of paper for placing inside this living Venn diagram.

- Now ask children to think of anything they might know about a whale or a dolphin and write it on a strip of paper.
- Gather children around the Venn diagram and ask a few children to place their strips of paper inside the circles.
- Look at the comments made. Do the rest of the class agree with the comments and where they have been placed? For example:

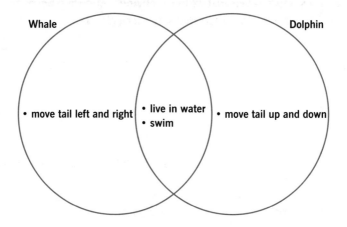

Whale | Dolphin

- move tail left and right
- live in water
- swim
- move tail up and down

- If children are struggling to think of ideas, write the following phrases onto the board and ask children to discuss where they would place them in the Venn diagram and how they would find out more about whales and dolphins to check.

  have a backbone, some hair on skin, breathe air with lungs, breathe air with gills, have fins, scaly skin, have a brain, have a heart, warm blooded, mostly cold blooded, most lay eggs, are mammals, nurse babies, are prehistoric.

- After children have talked about their ideas, place the words inside the Venn diagram and try to agree as a class where they should go.
- Ask children to draw their own Venn diagram for comparing cats and dogs and ask them to decide how the following characteristics should be placed:

  bark, meow, hunt for prey, sleep on windowsills and under cars, fleas, wear collars, don't come home when called, walk on a lead, like to be alone, often get lost, need to visit the vet, playful, come when called, like to climb, make good pets, groom themselves, will eat anything, need food and water, like to be with people, sleep on the floor and beds, bite, don't often get lost, bring you dead mice and birds, have tails.

Variations

- Invite children to use a Venn diagram to compare and contrast frogs and toads, a snake and a worm, a crocodile and an alligator, a butterfly and a moth, chimps and gorillas, a lion and a tiger, trees and flowers, flowering plants and non-flowering plants, insects and spiders, living and non-living things, teddy bears and real bears, fruit and vegetables, fresh water and salt water, healthy foods and snack foods, North Pole and South Pole, Earth and Moon, light and sound, push and pull, arteries and veins, a bird and an aeroplane, fire and water, vinegar and lemon juice, cat's eyes and cat's eyes (road).
- Venn diagrams can also compare three things. For example, three habitats could be put side by side and contrasted in a triple Venn like this one:

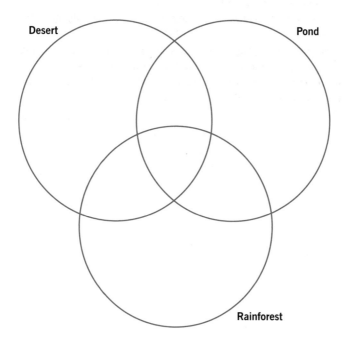

- You could compare and contrast four things using a graphic like the one below:

Venn diagram section (comparing 4 items)

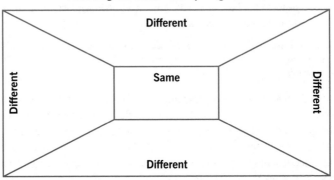

Challenge questions

- Can you write a science report for a newspaper or magazine using the information you have collected?
- Do circles or ellipses have to be used every time? Can you design a Venn diagram using other shapes and colours?
- Can you use a Venn diagram in other subjects to help you sort information? For example, to compare and contrast two or more authors?
- Can you find out more about the person who invented Venn diagrams?
- Can you design a Venn diagram with four circles?

Carroll diagrams

As an alternative to Venn diagrams you could use a Carroll diagram for sorting and representing information into groups or sets. Some Carroll diagrams use two boxes to compare and contrast, and others use four boxes or cells.

Suitable for

KS1
KS2

Aims

- To build on each other's contributions and chain them together into coherent lines of thinking.
- To build on previous knowledge and create new understanding.
- To share information and solve problems together.

Organisation

- This is suitable for small groups of two to four

Resources

- Carroll diagram templates

What to do

- Show children a simple Carroll diagram that compares two things in a simple table. Try to complete the following table together:

Plants that we can eat	Plants that we cannot eat
beetroot	grass
beansprouts	leaves from trees
rhubarb	flowers
spinach	weeds
watercress	
garlic	
cauliflower	

- Now show children another Carroll diagram and talk about how to complete it using the following words (these could be shown as pictures). Children may or may not agree with the choices already made and they can swap them if necessary.

    ant, house fly, head lice, wasp, daddy longlegs, cattle tick, grasshopper, silver fish, centipedes, cockroaches, dragonfly, mite, bee, butterfly, maggot, termite, mosquito, moth, greenfly, flea, bedbug, water boatman, leech, ladybird, bee, worm, snail.

	six legs	not six legs
wings	grasshopper, moth	daddy longlegs, ant
no wings	cockroach	maggot, caterpillar

- When children are familiar with the way a Carroll diagram works, complete another one together so they get used to filling them in. Here is another example relating to healthy eating:

	food I like	**food I don't like**
food I can eat a lot of	crisps, chicken	banana
food I should not eat a lot of	chips, cheese, tuna	

Variations

- Include 'bogus' words inside the Carroll diagrams so that children are challenged in their thinking.
- Include less obvious examples that fit a given criterion, so that children learn to question objects and ideas more thoughtfully. For example:

	magnetic	**not magnetic**
metal	tin foil, ruler, drinks can	drawing pin, calculator, glass
not a metal	cork, sugar	paperclip, salt, pencil

- You can compare and contrast literally hundreds of things. Why not think about trying a Carroll diagram for 'lives on water/does not live on water – has legs/has no legs'?

Challenge questions

- (Complete a Carroll diagram for another group and remove cell headings.) Can you work out what they are?
- (Complete a Carroll diagram for another group with the cell headings mixed up.) Can you work out their correct positions?
- Do you think Carroll diagrams are easier to use than Venn diagrams?

Branching diagrams

This graphic organiser shows the relationship between a complete object and its individual elements. Some of these parts may be vital to the function of the whole system, whereas some might not. It shows how a structure works and what is important in that system.

Suitable for

KS1
KS2

Aims

* To build on each other's contributions and chain them together into coherent lines of thinking.
* To build on previous knowledge and create new understanding.
* To share information and solve problems together.

Organisation

* This is suitable for small groups of two to four

Resources

* Branching graphic organiser template

What to do

* Explain to children what a branching diagram is, using a car as an example. Explain that the whole thing, in this case the car, is made up of many individual parts, some of which are essential to its function (steering mechanism, breaking mechanism, etc.), whereas other bits and pieces are not (doors, windows, etc.).

- To help children think about these parts, ask them to look at the branching graphic organiser below so they are able to see the connections and interrelatedness of components to the entirety and what would happen if some pieces were missing.

- Now show children another example of someone's understanding of a tulip (below) and its parts. Ask children to comment on the information written down. Would they change anything? What would they add?

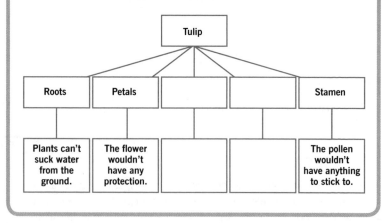

Variation

- Challenge children to invent their own branching graphic organiser and ask 'What is the whole object or concept?', 'What are the major parts of it?', 'What are the main jobs of its different parts?' Ideas to consider include an electrical circuit, a bicycle, a plug, a guitar, a seal, an elephant, the digestive system, and so on.

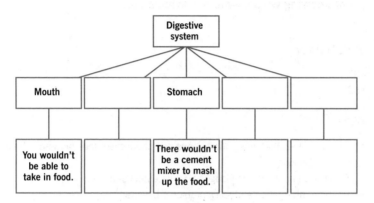

Challenge questions

- (Complete a diagram, removing the component part headings but keeping the information beneath them.) Can you work out what the individual part headings are?
- Can you complete a branching diagram for something that has ten parts?

The 5Ws and H grid

> The 5Ws and H grid is an information-gathering exercise for getting the 'full' story on something. This activity is good for knowing what's what and what's not!

Suitable for

KS1
KS2

Aims

- To build on each other's contributions and chain them together into coherent lines of thinking.
- To build on previous knowledge and create new understanding.
- To share information and solve problems together.

Organisation

- This is suitable for small groups of two to four

Resources

- 5Ws and H template

What to do

- Ask children to tell you what the 5W questions are and what the H stands for.
- Explain that these questions can be used to find out more about a topic, event, or incident.
- Teach children to ask more searching questions as follows:
    Who? Who was involved?
    What? What happened (what's the story)?

When? When did it take place?
Where? Where did it take place?
Why? Why did it happen?
How? How did it happen?

- Use a photograph as a starting point for practising the 5Ws and H. For example:

Who is involved?
Polar bears.

How many polar bears are left in the world? How can we stop their possible extinction?

Where is this happening? Where else do polar bears live? The Arctic circle.

What would polar bears say about this? What do they eat? What can we do to stop this happening?

When did this happen? It is happening now.

Why is this happening? Because of global warming.

- Go through each of the questions and ask children to volunteer any answers they may have that might be included in the boxes.

- Children can think of plenty more questions and then go away to find the answers to them.

Variations

- Look through some science news reports and copy and paste a picture into a grid like the previous example.
- You could use this graphic organiser to evaluate a science webpage or a dictionary. For example:

  Who? Who wrote the pages and are they an expert?
  What? What else might the author have included?
  When? When was the site last updated?
  Where? Where does the information come from?
  Why? Why is this page better than another?

- The 5Ws and H format can also be presented as a wheel or a pyramid.

Challenge questions

- Can you write a news scoop for a newspaper or website using the 5Ws and H as an inverted pyramid as follows?

Headline			
Who?	What?	Where?	When?
	Why?	How?	
	Detail		

- Can you work in pairs to conduct mock interviews to help complete the pyramid?

Word wheel

Word wheel is a simple and effective graphic useful for kick-starting thinking about a topic or object and assessing knowledge and understanding.

Suitable for

KS1
KS2

Aims

- To build on each other's contributions and chain them together into coherent lines of thinking.
- To build on previous knowledge and create new understanding.
- To share information and solve problems together.

Organisation

- This is suitable for small groups of two to four

Resources

- Word wheel template

What to do

- Ask children to close their eyes and visualise an apple. How would they describe it?
- Using the word wheel, ask children to use as many words as possible to describe what an apple looks like, what it feels like, what it smells of and what it tastes of. Emphasise that you are looking for colourful and exciting adjectives to paint a picture of the apple.

- A completed example might look like this:

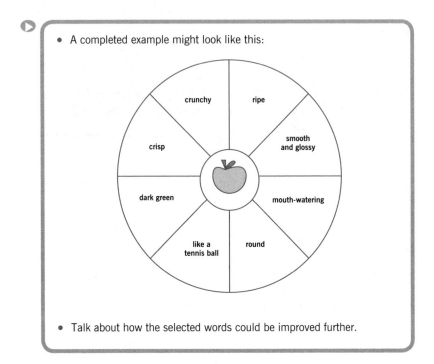

- Talk about how the selected words could be improved further.

Variations

- Children could go on to create a science poem, using their words as inspiration. For example:

    Crunch!
    The ripe tennis ball of nature.
    Crisp, sweet and tastebud friendly.
    Keeps the doctor at bay.

- Think of other objects to go inside the word wheel. You could choose another fruit, a leaf, the heart, the Moon, a rock, teeth, a habitat, an animal and so on.

Challenge questions

- Can you include more sections inside the word wheel?
- Can you write a story going around the wheel in a clockwise direction, using the words to describe your chosen object?
- Can you write an acrostic using the words inside your wheel?

Sunshine webs

Sunshine or star webs are really useful for basic brainstorming about a topic. They can be used to describe what children know about a topic.

Suitable for

KS1
KS2

Aims

- To build on each other's contributions and chain them together into coherent lines of thinking.
- To build on previous knowledge and create new understanding.
- To share information and solve problems together.

Organisation

- This is suitable for small groups of two to four

Resources

- Sunshine web templates

What to do

- With this graphic organiser, children should write a name or concept word in the centre circle and any associated ideas and details that they can think of in the smaller circles (these can be any number you choose).

- For example, you might be looking at living things in their environment and how animals are adapted to their habitat. Place the word 'camel' in the centre circle and see if children can think of any special features a camel has developed to live in the desert. The following graphic organiser has almost been completed.

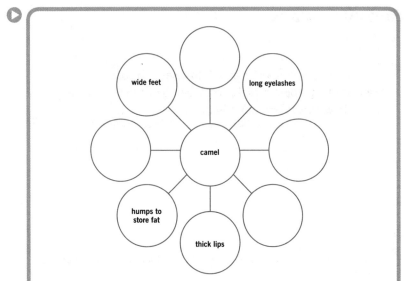

- This idea is particularly useful for brainstorming about the senses: smell-related words, taste-related words, hearing-related words, sight-related words, and touch-related words. One example is taste. When children have completed their star web they can compare and contrast their ideas with another group, or find synonyms that mean the same thing.

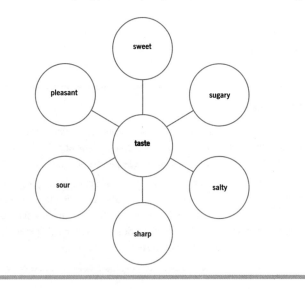

Variation

- Try this idea for an otter, penguin, desert rat, squirrel, frog or cactus. You could also try this for animals, groups, sounds, light, materials, separating mixtures and so on. Some star webs can be split off into smaller stars of their own.

Challenge questions

- Can you draw smaller circles coming out of the larger circles to add further ideas and descriptions to your sunshine web?
- Can you write associated ideas on the lines joining the circles?
- Can you combine your ideas with those of another group to create an upgraded web?

Word maps

Word maps challenge children to write what they know about a key concept. Children are asked to think of their own definition and then compare that to a dictionary definition. They then think of a word connected to the key word, a clue word and an associated picture.

Suitable for

KS1
KS2

Aims

- To build on each other's contributions and chain them together into coherent lines of thinking.
- To build on previous knowledge and create new understanding.
- To share information and solve problems together.

Organisation

- This is suitable for small groups of two to four

Resources

- Word map template

What to do

- Show children the 'friction' example on page 83 to illustrate how a word map works. Explain that they are designed to help children make connections, build vocabulary and improve their scientific word power.
- Go through each of the categories and ask children to help you complete the map.

- Talk about how to improve the word map and make revisions where appropriate.

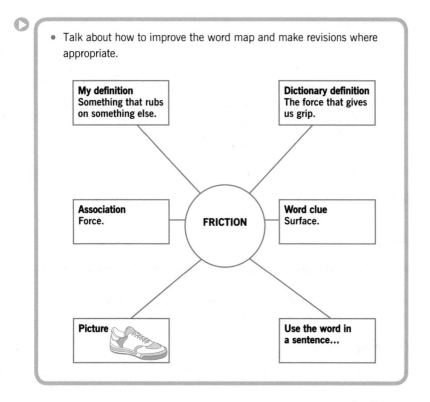

Variations

- You can adapt the categories given: for example, 'word used in a paragraph', 'word used in a newspaper', 'word used in everyday life', 'web definitions' and so on.
- Children can turn the word map into a poster and use it as a part of a display.
- Individual words in a topic can be mapped by different groups rather than the whole class focusing on one key concept.

Challenge questions

- What other categories could you add to a word map?
- Can you create a mini revision guide by writing different word maps for different topics?

Spidergrams

> A spidergram or spider diagram is a type of graphic organiser that is used to explore various aspects of a single topic, helping children to organise their thoughts.

Suitable for

KS1
KS2

Aims

- To build on each other's contributions and chain them together into coherent lines of thinking.
- To build on previous knowledge and create new understanding.
- To share information and solve problems together.

Organisation

- This is suitable for small groups of two to four

Resources

- Spidergram template
- Fishbone template

What to do

- Show children the example of a spidergram below – of spiders! Do they agree with what has been written?
- Some of the information is not correct – can they spot it or find out more? For example: not all spiders have eight legs; spiders are not insects, not all spiders make webs; some female spiders eat the male after mating; some baby spiders eat the mother spiders as they grow up.

- Challenge children to think of more words connected to the main word.

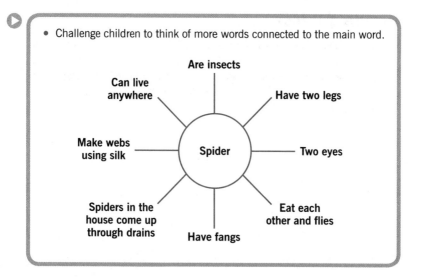

Variations

- You can limit the number of legs, or increase them.
- Use a picture in the centre instead of a word.
- Ask children to write a sentence at the end of each leg instead of a word.
- Present the information given as a fishbone/herringbone map.

For example:

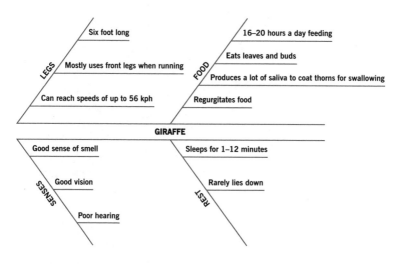

Challenge questions

- Show children a science video clip and ask if they can work in pairs to create a spider diagram using the information shown.
- Read a passage from a science text twice and ask children to complete a spider diagram using the information shared. Do the children's diagrams agree with each other?

Cycle diagrams

Cycle diagrams shows how things are linked to one another in a repeating cycle. You would use a cycle diagram when there is no beginning and no end to a repeating process.

Suitable for

KS1
KS2

Aims

- To build on each other's contributions and chain them together into coherent lines of thinking.
- To build on previous knowledge and create new understanding.
- To share information and solve problems together.

Organisation

- This is suitable for small groups of two to four

Resources

- Cycle diagram

What to do

- Look at the cycle diagram on page 86 together.
- Explain that information is presented inside squares or circles and these are numbered to show where a process starts and ends.
- Warn children that the stages can be deliberately mixed up, though.
- Explain that how many squares or circles you use will depend on the number of stages in the cycle you are looking at. For example, the lunar cycle or rock cycle will have more stages than the life cycle of a grasshopper.

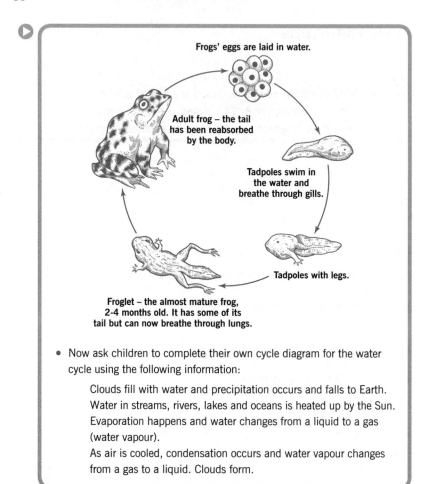

Frogs' eggs are laid in water.

Adult frog – the tail has been reabsorbed by the body.

Tadpoles swim in the water and breathe through gills.

Tadpoles with legs.

Froglet – the almost mature frog, 2-4 months old. It has some of its tail but can now breathe through lungs.

- Now ask children to complete their own cycle diagram for the water cycle using the following information:

  Clouds fill with water and precipitation occurs and falls to Earth. Water in streams, rivers, lakes and oceans is heated up by the Sun. Evaporation happens and water changes from a liquid to a gas (water vapour).

  As air is cooled, condensation occurs and water vapour changes from a gas to a liquid. Clouds form.

Variations

- These graphics can be presented in words, pictures or both.
- There are lots of life cycles that children can go away and research: a shark, a fly, an Alaska salmon, stars, jellyfish, biennial and perennial plants, bedbugs, a salamander, a Monarch butterfly and so on.

Challenge questions

- Can you find out what happens if one stage of a cycle is interfered with in some way? Can the cycle continue?
- Can you write about a cycle of events from the point of view of the animal involved?

Matching

Matching graphic organisers display information in a simple table. Children can be presented with these to number in pencil and say which word matches which definition. Connecting with lines tends to be too messy.

Suitable for

KS1
KS2

Aims

- To build on each other's contributions and chain them together into coherent lines of thinking.
- To build on previous knowledge and create new understanding.
- To share information and solve problems together.

Organisation

- This is suitable for small groups of two to four

Resources

- Matching templates

What to do

- Show children the first table on page 90 and explain that the information has been mixed up and you need their help to sort it out.

Animal	Food	What helps it to feed
shark	fruit	sticky web made of silk
giraffe	rabbits	hands
crab	flies	long sticky tongue
eagle	leaves	very strong beak
snake	ants and grubs	sharp teeth
spider	dead fish	curved sharp talons
parrot	penguins	large strong claws
mussel	rats	very long neck
monkey	nuts	fangs and poison
green woodpecker	microscopic animals	tiny hairs to filter water

- Give children another table to match animals with the food they might eat and what they use to help them to eat. For example:

Animal	Food	What helps it to feed
shark		
giraffe		
crab		
eagle		
snake		
spider		
parrot		
mussel		
monkey		
green woodpecker		

Variations

- Another way to present a matching activity is to use matching cards such as those below. Give children a set of cards per table group and ask them to work out what word matches which definition. The cards can be cut up and placed side by side.

Dissolve	A very fine sieve. The paper holds back the pieces of undissolved liquid. while letting the liquid through.
Solution	It can be poured and takes the shape of the container it is in.
Melt	To change from liquid to solid.
Solidify	Changes from a liquid to a gas.
Freeze	A material that keeps it shape.
Filter	To change from solid to liquid.
Solid	Solid in liquid. or liquid in liquid.
Liquid	When two materials are totally mixed.
Soluble	To change state from liquid to solid. usually at low temperatures.

Evaporation	A substance that dissolves in water.
Condensation	When a gas cools to form a liquid.

- You could play this game as a loop activity where children call out the concept and whoever has the matching definition puts their hand up, reads it out and then calls out their definition.

Challenge questions

- Can you create your own matching activity for another group to try.
- Can you write a set of matching cards on the same topic but for different age groups, changing the words to match level of understanding?

T-charts

> T-charts asks children to use a type of graphic organiser to list and explore two ideas within a topic. This might be something like facts and opinions, pros and cons, advantages and disadvantages, or listing two characteristics of a new topic.

Suitable for

KS1
KS2

Aims

- To build on each other's contributions and chain them together into coherent lines of thinking.
- To build on previous knowledge and create new understanding.
- To share information and solve problems together.

Organisation

- This is suitable for small groups of two to four

Resources

- T-chart template

What to do

- Explain what a T-chart is and show children the chart example on page 94 about changes in matter. The chart distinguishes between examples of physical changes and chemical changes.

- Explain that the table has been completed by another class and you want them to check it. Which changes do they agree have been correctly chosen? Can they think of any more?

Physical changes	Chemical changes
You freeze some water.	You burn a piece of paper.
You break a glass.	You mix vinegar with bicarbonate of soda.
You dissolve some coffee in hot water.	You leave a piece of bread to go mouldy.
Your trousers get ripped.	Your clothes get wet.
You paint a door.	You open a bottle of lemonade.
You light a candle.	You leave your bike outside to get rusty.
You fold some paper to make an origami boat.	You leave some milk out of the fridge for two days.

- Focus on any disagreements and change the T-chart so that it is accurate.
- Fill in the rest of the chart with more examples.

Variation

- Using another partially completed T-chart, present it to children without the headings – can children think of what the headings might be?

Challenge questions

- Can you turn a T-chart into a debate between two example ideas, evaluating the pros and cons of each?
- Can you write a balanced report comparing and contrasting the objects in your T-chart?

Y-charts

Y-charts are graphic organisers that use three senses to classify information. They can be used to help children organise what they know about an object, topic or idea by writing and drawing what it looks like, sounds like, smells like, tastes like or feels like (just three of these are chosen).

Suitable for

KS1
KS2

Aims

- To build on each other's contributions and chain them together into coherent lines of thinking.
- To build on previous knowledge and create new understanding.
- To share information and solve problems together.

Organisation

- This is suitable for small groups of two to four

Resources

- Y-chart template

What to do

- Show children an example of a Y-chart (see page 96) and point out the questions asked within it: What does it look like? What does it sound like? What does it feel like?

Earthworm:

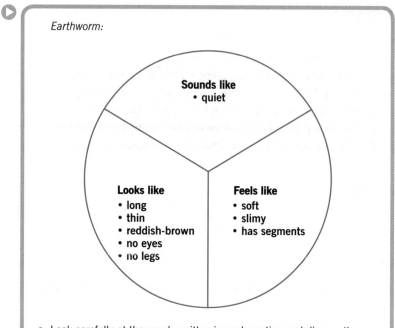

- Look carefully at the words written in each section and discuss them in pairs. Are they accurate? Can any be improved and rewritten? Are there more words to add?

- Let children share their ideas with the class.

- Give children access to books and the internet so they can find out more in order to add to the Y-chart.

Variations

- Have different groups working on different insects or animals rather than the same one.
- Change one of the senses for something else: for example, what does it smell like?

Challenge questions

- Can you invent your own Y-chart for describing three aspects of a topic to include new observations or characteristics?
- Can you write a poem based on the information you collect for your Y-chart?

ADI tables

> ADI tables are graphic organisers that help children think about the advantages and disadvantages of a topic and some interesting things associated with a particular topic.

Suitable for

KS1
KS2

Aims

- To build on each other's contributions and chain them together into coherent lines of thinking.
- To build on previous knowledge and create new understanding.
- To share information and solve problems together.

Organisation

- This is suitable for small groups of two to four

Resources

- ADI table template

What to do

- Show children the ADI table on page 98 and explain what each of the letters stands for.
- Explain that the table asks children to think about the pros and cons of caring for their teeth. What do they think about the ideas shown?

Advantages	Disadvantages	Interesting points
Brushing your teeth protects them from decay.	Brushing your teeth too long and too hard ruins the enamel on your teeth.	You need to brush your tongue to get rid of bacteria.
Brushing your teeth makes them stronger.	Brushing too hard can cause receding gums and tooth sensitivity.	Before toothpaste was invented, people used all kinds of dry, rough things as an abrasive to clean their teeth – things like crushed eggshell, pumice and the burnt hooves of animals!
Brushing your teeth keeps gums healthy.	Brushing gums can make them bleed.	Before toothbrushes were invented people used twigs or their fingers to brush their teeth.
Brushing with a tooth whitening paste makes your teeth whiter and shinier.	Tooth whitening paste can damage your teeth and gums.	Each day, the average person spends 8.5 hours sleeping, 1 hour eating, 7.2 minutes volunteering and only 50 seconds brushing their teeth.
Mouthwash helps keep your mouth clean.	Some alcohol-based mouth washes can cause cancer of the mouth.	

- Now share another ADI table with children and challenge groups to complete the gaps. On page 99 is an example about exercising; explain that some of the boxes have been started but need completing too.

Advantages	Disadvantages	Interesting points
Become fitter.	Increased risk of injury.	Your muscles don't get bigger during exercise. They strengthen when you are resting.
Good for your ...	Could have a ... ... if you do too much.	A person can be overweight and fit.
Improves your ...	Could become ... to exercise.	
	Could harm your ... system.	
Sleep better.		

- Invite children to discuss their ideas and present a list to the class.

Variation

- Think of other ADI tables. Possible ideas include what would happen if door handles were made of chocolate, books were made of rubber, curtains were made of paper, gravity was stronger, magnetism was weaker, and so on.

Challenge questions

- Hold a debate in relation to the question being asked. Can children argue the pros and cons convincingly enough to persuade another group either way?
- Do advantages and disadvantages hold equal weighting in an argument? Look at your completed ADI table and decide which advantages and disadvantages are more persuasive than others.

Q·charts

Q-charts provide a framework for creating questions and are excellent ways to improve children's enquiry skills and extend their thinking skills.

Suitable for

KS1
KS2

Aims

- To build on each other's contributions and chain them together into coherent lines of thinking.
- To build on previous knowledge and create new understanding.
- To share information and solve problems together.

Organisation

- This is suitable for small groups of two to four

Resources

- Q-chart template

What to do

- Children use the grid by starting with a word from the first column and then adding a verb from the top row. The combination you choose will drive your question and not all boxes will need to be completed. The further down and to the right you go, the more complex and high-level the questions. Factual questions tend to be what/where/when/who is/ did/can? Prediction-based questions tend to be what/where/when/who would/will/might? Analytical question are of the sort why/how is/did/ can? Synthesis/application questions are why/how would/will/might?

- Show children the following example about solids, liquids and gases, and challenge them to add ideas of their own.

	is/as/are	do/did/does	can/could	would	will	might
Who						Who might study solids, liquids and gases for a job?
What	What is the most common state of matter in the universe – solid, liquid or gas?	What do we call lemonade if it is a liquid and a gas?		What would you call glass – a solid or a liquid?		
Where		Where does the liquid come from on the outside of a cold glass of water?				
When			When could an aerosol be classed as a solid, a liquid and a gas?	When would a solid behave like a liquid?		
How		How can you tell the difference between gases if they are invisible?				
Why	Why is oil classed as a liquid when it could solidify?	Why does helium allow an airship to float? Why do solids melt?				Why might nitrogen be a liquid and a gas?

- When questions have been posed, different groups could then be given the task of researching them to feedback to the rest of the class.

Variations

- Reduce the number of question categories or add more as appropriate.
- Present a blank grid for challenging your most able pupils.

Challenge questions

- Can you make a list of other question stems that would help to find out more about a particular idea or topic?
- Can you select some questions and post them to a scientist to answer in person by visiting your school?

Analogy graphics

Analogy graphics help children to learn and connect new concepts. Children link new ideas by comparing them to concepts they are already familiar with.

Suitable for

KS1
KS2

Aims

- To build on each other's contributions and chain them together into coherent lines of thinking.
- To build on previous knowledge and create new understanding.
- To share information and solve problems together.

Organisation

- This is suitable for small groups of two to four

Resources

- Analogy templates

What to do

- Explain to children that the world of science and invention is filled with discoveries made through analogous thinking. Velcro, for instance, was developed after someone examined the hooks on a burr.
- Explain that analogous thinking means that you can think of parts of one thing and compare these to the parts of another: for example, a cat and a car.

Cat	Car
head	bonnet
eye	headlight
mouth	fuel cap
stomach	fuel tank
skeleton	chassis
heart	engine
paw	wheel
fur	paint
bottom	exhaust pipe

- Ask children to think about how two things that seem unconnected might be alike. For example, how is a dishwasher like a tree? At first it might seem as though these two things have nothing in common but, after some creative thinking and prompting, children should be able to generate some ideas.
- Try challenging children to think how the seasons are like a circus/ riding a bike/a dance/an alarm clock. Possible responses might include:

  They both take you into new terrain.
  They both follow a trail.
  No matter how many times you go on a bike ride or through a season, you notice something new.
  You end up where you started.
  You can get weary of riding and tired of winter.
  They both take some work to prepare for.

Variation

- Children could present their ideas using a format such as the following:

Blood and ketchup

Blood is like ketchup because ...
1. they are both red.
2. they both contain sugar.
3. they are both manmade.
4.
5.

A dishwasher and a tree

A dishwasher is like a tree because ...
1. they both need water.
2. they both clean things.
3. they both follow a cycle.
4.
5.

A hotdog and a shoe

A hotdog is like a shoe because ...
1. they are both long and thin.
2. they are made from animals.
3. they both go with another object.
4.
5.

Challenge questions

- Can you write a story using personification to highlight how one object is like another?
- Can you find out more about other scientific discoveries that have been made by analogous thinking?

Acrostic summary grid

Acrostic summary grid involves writing a key concept down the page of a grid and challenges children to complete it with associated sentences that illustrate central ideas, perhaps using examples.

Suitable for

KS1
KS2

Aims

- To build on each other's contributions and chain them together into coherent lines of thinking.
- To build on previous knowledge and create new understanding.
- To share information and solve problems together.

Organisation

- This is suitable for small groups of two to four.

Resources

- Acrostic summary template

What to do

- Children will be familiar with acrostics already, but recap for anyone who is unsure.
- Explain that you want children to read the piece of text about habitats on page 108 and then present some of the information from that text in an acrostic summary grid.

Almost everywhere in the world is a home to at least one type of living thing. The area where a plant or animal lives is called its habitat. It is a place where an animal or plant finds water, food, shelter and some protection from its enemies.

Some habitats are large like a rainforest, the Arctic, or an ocean. Others are quite small, such as a spot of pond water, or a rotten log. Many living things depend in some way on one another, making up a large living family or community.

Each living thing is well suited to live in a particular environment. Animals can live in many different places in the world because they have special adaptations to the area that they live in.

An adaptation is a way an animal's body helps it survive, or live, in its environment. For example, a polar bear (the largest land carnivore) has white fur to help it blend in with the snowy Arctic icelands. However, a polar bear's skin is actually black, which allows it to soak up as much heat as possible from the sun. It has large, wide paws to help it to walk in the snow.

Examples of the basic adaptations that help creatures survive include:

- *the shape of a bird's beak*
- *the number of fingers*
- *the colour of the fur*
- *the thickness or thinness of the fur*
- *the shape of the nose or ears.*

Each adaptation has been produced by evolution. This means that the adaptations have developed over many generations. But what would happen if animals changed habitats? Could a walrus live in a desert, or a rattlesnake live in the Arctic?

- A completed example of an acrostic summary grid is given opposite:

H	Home for plants and animals where they find water, food, shelter and protection.
A	Adapted to their environment.
B	Blending into their surroundings (for example, a polar bear's white fur).
I	It has large, wide paws to help it walk in the snow.
T	Their skin is actually black to absorb the sun.
A	And it has large white paws for walking on the ice.
T	The largest land carnivore in the snowy Arctic lands.

Challenge questions

- What would happen if the animals switched habitats?
- What adaptation features would be useful or useless in the new habitat?
- Do you think the animal could survive in the unfamiliar habitat?
- What does that tell you about how animals adapt to their environments?
- Can you write an acrostic poem using more than one sentence per letter?
- Can you finish your sentence beginning with the next letter of your acrostic letter?
- Can you write a double acrostic poem where each line begins and ends with the same subject letter? For example, CAT might look like:

> Creates a lot of havoc
> Attacking bowls of semolina
> Tearing up my T-shirt

Chapter 3

Life processes and living things - experiments

'When you breathe, you inspire. When you do not breathe, you expire.'

Clever potatoes

Clever potatoes is an experiment to show the effect of light on plant growth.

Theme

Green plants

Suitable for

KS1
KS2

Aim

- To recognise that plants need light and water to grow.

Resources

- Small plant pot
- Potting mix
- Shoebox
- Several sheets of thick cardboard
- Sticky tape
- Sprouting potatoes

What to do

- Cut a small hole in one end of a shoebox.
- Place a potato in a small plant pot containing potting mix, sprouts side up.
- Place the plant pot at the opposite end of the shoebox from the light hole.
- Cut the cardboard into strips and use the pieces to create an obstacle course between the potato and the hole.

- Put your box in a sunny position with the hole facing the light.
- Observe the growth of the potato every day, making sure to put the lid back on tightly.
- As this is an experiment to do over time, you will need to chart its progress each week. As time goes on, you will see that the potato sprouts grow around the obstacle course to get to the light.
- At the end of the investigation, explain to the children what is happening: plants need sunlight and oxygen so they can produce food in a process called photosynthesis. Plants in darker surroundings will generally grow towards the light to increase their photosynthesising potential.

Variations

- You could try this experiment with different potatoes.
- Try experimenting with other plants. Ask questions such as 'Do all plants grow the same way?'

Challenge questions

- Did the potato need water to grow?
- Would the type of compost used matter?
- Does the compost used need to be damp or dry?
- Have you ever wondered how a weed, poking through a pavement crack, or a bit of driveway, can seemingly pop up through concrete? Can you explain how this happens, based on what you know about the experiment above?
- Does the time of the year when you carry out this experiment make a difference?

Safety consideration

- Children should wash hands after handling soil and compost.

Tasty

Tasty is an enjoyable taste-testing activity that helps children recognise the important role their senses play.

Theme

Humans and other animals

Suitable for

KS1
KS2

Aims

- To identify the five senses and location of the sense organs.
- To develop the skills of speaking and listening and expressing ideas through a variety of media.

Resources

- Five flavours of crisps
- Five bowls
- Sticky labels

What to do

- Collect together five bowls and put five different flavours of crisps inside each of them. You can mark the flavours by writing the description on a sticky label underneath each bowl.
- Tell children that their job is to taste the crisps and guess the flavour in each bowl.
- Children can record their ideas on a piece of paper as they taste each flavour.
- At the end of the taste test, children can see whether they were right or not when you reveal the true identity of each flavour.

Variations

- To vary the experiment, tell children to hold their noses and close their eyes when they do a taste test. Talk about how removing the sense of smell makes it more difficult to put a name to the flavour.
- You could try other foods, such as different flavours of yoghurt, fruit, fruit juices, and fruit gums.
- Add different quantities of sugar to cups containing the same amount of water. Ask children to taste the sweetness of each one.

Challenge questions

- Why might blindfolding or closing eyes make a difference to the outcome of the taste test?
- Can you think of other kinds of taste test?
- How can the taste tests be made fair?

Safety considerations

- Before tasting food, make sure children wash their hands and that bowls and tables are clean.
- Check that children do not have any food allergies.
- Remind children never to taste an unknown substance.

Chewing the fat

Chewing the fat is an experiment to illustrate the fat content in different foods.

Theme

Teeth and eating

Suitable for

KS1
KS2

Aim

- To identify how much fat there is in the food we eat.

Resources

- Different foods to test, such as crisps, salami, samosas, chips, a baked potato, peanuts, peanut butter, an apple, a banana, a burger
- Brown paper grocery bags or brown paper
- Butter

What to do

- Ask children if they have ever eaten fat before. Ask which foods they think contain fat. Ask how to spot a fatty food from a non-fatty food.
- Take a brown paper bag and rub a small amount of butter on the bag. What do children now notice about the bag? Is the bag opaque, translucent or transparent?
- Show children the other foods you are going to test. Can they predict which ones will have the most fat? About 90 per cent of the fat we eat comes from three categories of food: fats and oils; meat, poultry and fish; and dairy foods. Fruits and vegetables (with the exception

of olives and avocados) and grains are very low in fat. Foods that are low in fat can become a high fat food because of the way they are processed. For example, since potato chips are fried in fat, they are higher in fat than baked potatoes.

- Test the foods for fat by doing the same grease spot test and then look to see which foods have the most fat and the least fat.
- Ask children to try this test at home using different foods.

Variations

- Before the food experiment, ask children to rub their fingers across a brown paper bag – is there any fat on their fingers? Have children washed their hands?
- Repeat the experiment and leave the brown paper bags overnight – the next day you will see which foods have the most fat.
- Test foods from different outlets to see the fat content difference. For example, you could test a burger from four different burger restaurants.
- Ask children to think of other ways of testing for fats.

Challenge questions

- How can you make this a fair test? For example, think about the brown paper bag – does it need to be the same size each time? How long do you rub the food on the bag for?
- What do you notice about the paper that fish and chips are wrapped in? Can you tell how much fat they might contain?
- Discuss why fat is important to our diet and also harmful to our health. What different types of fat are there?

Safety consideration

- Hand hygiene is important both before and after this experiment.

Salt of the Earth

Salt of the Earth is a very engaging investigation to illustrate the salt content of crisps. It highlights the vigilance necessary when eating foods that may contain lots of salt.

Theme

Humans and other animals

Suitable for

KS1
KS2

Aim

- To show that foods contain salt, which can be harmful to health if eaten in large quantities.

Resources

- Different varieties of ready salted crisps
- Microscopes

What to do

- Divide children up into small mixed-ability groups.
- Give each group three bags of ready salted crisps and a microscope.
- Ask children to compare how much salt each bag has by using the microscope to look at the salt visible on the crisps from the different packets.
- Ask the children to taste the crisps – can they spot the difference between them?
- Encourage children to be canny consumers by reading the labels on the back of each packet so they can spot the salt content and make a healthy choice when choosing a bag of crisps. Eighty-five per cent

of the salt we eat is hidden in processed or takeaway foods, rather than added at the table. Many food packets talk about sodium content rather than salt content. Help children to make sense of this – every gram of sodium is equivalent to 2.5g of salt.

- Discuss why too much salt can be bad for you. For example, excessive salt is a major cause of strokes and heart attacks, the two major causes of death in the UK.

- Look at the salt content of a variety of other food labels. Tell children that some ready-made sandwiches can contain as much salt as seven bags of crisps.

Variation

- Conduct a taste test before the experiment. Call each bag Bag A, Bag B, Bag C and have some children taste a crisp from each bag. Can they work out which is the saltiest? Tell children to have a sip of water between each taste.

Challenge questions

- Is a taste test more accurate than looking at the nutritional information on the back of a bag of crisps? Discuss the fact that taste perceptions differ and can be unreliable.
- Can you think of five different ways of comparing the amount of salt in different crisps?
- Could you separate the salt from the crisps? For example, what about washing the salt off, filtering and evaporating? Could you weigh the salt?
- An investigation has found that breakfast cereals marketed at children contain more sugar per serving than a jam doughnut. Can you plan a fair test investigation into how much sugar breakfast cereals contain in a similar way to the crisp test?
- Why do manufacturers of foods put so much salt into foods? (For example, it can be used to bind water into meats, salt adds flavour to food and salt makes you thirsty!)
- Can you find out what is the daily recommended allowance of salt for adults and children?
- Can you find out about National Salt Awareness Week on the internet?

Safety consideration

- When taste testing, remember good hand hygiene.

Eat your reds

> Eat your reds is a very simple and fun science experiment to show how a plant absorbs water and transports it.

Theme

Green plants

Suitable for

KS1
KS2

Aim

- To show that water and minerals are taken in through the root and transported through the stem to other parts of the plant.

Resources

- Celery stalks with leaves
- One tablespoon (15 millilitres) of red food colouring, paint powder or coloured ink
- Two tall, clear jars
- Water
- Chopping board and knife

What to do

- Pour some water into both jars or containers. Ask children to consider whether the type of water – still or fizzy, hard or soft – would make a difference to the experiment.
- Add a tablespoon of food colouring to the water in one of the jars.
- Stand the celery in the jars.

- Wait 24 hours. Ask children to predict what will have happened to the celery.
- Remove the celery stalk from the cup and cut one centimetre off the bottom. Look for small circles at the bottom of the stalk – they will be the colour of the food colouring you used.

Variations

- Repeat the experiment using other colours – ask children if they think people would buy different colours of celery. Discuss trying to sell the new colour range to a supermarket.
- Repeat the experiment using different fluids, such as orange juice, cola, tea and so on.
- Try hot and cold water to see if this influences the result.
- Try the experiment using a white carnation. Split the flower's stem lengthways so that you have three stems. Put each stem into a different beaker of coloured water (red, blue, green) and see what happens. One third will turn red, one third blue and one third green.
- This experiment could lead into cross-curricular work about tie-dye.

Challenge questions

- Does the height of a plant affect how it moves water?
- Does the temperature of the room make a difference? Try the carnation experiment with two flowers and in two different environments.
- Do all plants and animals work in the same way? If a chicken is fed on sweetcorn then the skin is often yellow. Would this happen to humans?

Safety consideration

- An adult must be responsible for all knife-cutting.

Rotten luck

Rotten luck is an effective little experiment that shows the effects of acid on teeth without actually damaging any teeth in the process!

Theme

Nutrition

Suitable for

KS1
KS2

Aim

- To show that acid can be harmful to teeth.

Resources

- Large bottle of cola
- Plastic drinks containers
- White-shelled hard-boiled eggs
- Old toothbrush
- Fluoride toothpaste
- Timer or clock

What to do

- Before doing the experiment, ask children to think about in what ways an eggshell is like our teeth. Discuss as a class.
- Fill the containers with cola and give each child an egg and a container. Ask children to place the egg in the container.
- Ask children to discuss what they think will happen to the egg over a period of time.
- Leave the egg for 30 minutes to an hour. Children can then remove the egg – what do they notice? The egg will have turned a brown colour.

- Now get children to use a toothbrush and toothpaste to brush the egg back to its original colour.
- Explain to children what has happened and discuss together the importance of good oral hygiene:

Sugar (in the cola) combines with bacteria in your mouth to form acid. This acid attacks our teeth. Over time, these acid attacks weaken tooth enamel (the hard outer covering of your teeth), causing discolouration of our teeth, as well as creating holes called cavities. The fluoride treatment protects the egg's shell from the acid. Our teeth need to be protected from the acids in our mouths with fluoride too. In order to keep our teeth healthy, we need to keep them clean by brushing with a toothpaste that contains fluoride and by flossing regularly.

Variations

- You could cover an egg in fluoride toothpaste and place that in cola to compare it to an untreated egg.
- Hang a piece of eggshell from a thread and suspend it in a beaker of cola. Do this in beakers of other liquids too, such as squash, water, fresh fruit juice and coffee. Leave them for a week and study the eggshell fragments for comparison.
- Put an egg in vinegar and leave it for a day. Take it out and feel it. Then leave the egg sitting out on a table for another day and then feel it again. Can children explain what happens? You could try the same experiment with chicken bones.
- Invite a dentist or oral hygienist into school to talk about tooth decay. Perhaps you could ask a dentist to bring in some real sterilised teeth for doing the experiment again.

Challenge questions

- What would happen if you did the experiments above in different environments? Would that make a difference?
- What is calcium carbonate? Look it up in a science dictionary.
- What substances contain calcium carbonate?
- Do all eggs have hard shells? Find out about the eggs of amphibians such as frogs and toads. Find out about the eggs of reptiles such as snakes and tortoises.

Safety considerations

- Make sure that the eggs are cleaned thoroughly before use, or handle them using plastic gloves.
- Dispose of broken eggs safely. Children should not touch raw egg, and should wear plastic gloves to clear away.

Magic balloons

Magic balloons is an engaging activity to help children understand the science of bread making by making a yeast-air balloon.

Theme

Nutrition

Suitable for

KS1
KS2

Aims

- To describe that yeast requires sugar and warmth to grow/reproduce.
- To understand that because microbes are living, they are useful in some food production.

Resources

- Packets of active dry yeast
- Flask of very warm water
- Sugar
- Some large rubber balloons
- Some one-litre empty water bottles

What to do

- Distribute the materials to small groups of children.
- Fill up the water bottles with about 3–4 cm of warm water. Explain that when yeast is cold or dry, the micro-organisms are resting.
- Now ask children to add the contents of a yeast packet and gently swirl the bottle a few seconds. Explain that as the yeast dissolves, it becomes active – it comes to life!

- Now ask children to add a small amount of sugar and swirl the water around some more. Explain that the yeast is now feeding.
- Ask children to blow up their balloon a few times to stretch it out, then to place the neck of the balloon over the neck of the bottle.
- Leave the bottle to sit in a warm place for about 20 minutes.
- The balloons should begin to inflate after a while.
- Talk about what has happened: as the yeast feeds on the sugar, it produces carbon dioxide. With no place to go but up, this gas slowly fills the balloon. A very similar process happens as bread rises. Carbon dioxide from yeast forms thousands of balloon-like bubbles in the dough. This is what gives the baked loaf its airy texture.

Variations

- Try the same experiment, but this time use about a tablespoon of baking powder instead of yeast, and leave out the sugar. What differences do you notice?
- Try the same experiment using hotter and then colder water. Use a thermometer to measure the temperature of the water. At what temperature is the yeast most active? At what temperatures is it unable to blow up the balloon?

Challenge questions

- Does room temperature affect how much gas is created by the yeast?
- Does the size of the container affect how much gas is created?
- Does the shape and material of the balloon make a difference?
- What water helps the yeast create the most gas?
- What yeast food helps the yeast create the most gas? For example, instead of sugar, what about honey or syrup?

Safety considerations

- There is a danger that the balloons could pop if too much carbon dioxide is produced. Limit the ingredients accordingly.
- Tie an elastic band around the neck of the bottle and balloon to avoid accidents.

Stomach churning

> Stomach churning is a hands-on activity for demonstrating how food is digested.

Theme

Nutrition

Suitable for

KS1
KS2

Aim

- To understand about the need for food for activity and growth, and about the importance of an adequate and varied diet for health.

Resources

- Bread
- Bananas
- Knife
- Potato mashers
- Water
- Vinegar
- Red and blue food colouring
- Washing up-liquid
- Large bowls
- Aprons
- Plastic bag

What to do

- Cover the tables in newspaper and distribute the materials to each small group. Children should wear aprons to protect their clothes.
- Challenge children to think about what happens when you chew, swallow and digest your food.
- Tell them that you are going to show them what happens when we eat a sandwich, using the materials in front of them (go through what each table should have).
- Ask children to peel and slice the banana and place between two slices of bread. To illustrate the incisors cutting the food, children should cut the bread into pieces using a knife. (Supervise the use of knives closely to avoid accidents.)
- Now put the sandwich pieces into a bowl and, using a potato masher demonstrate the molars grinding the food.
- Add some water and red food colouring to represent the saliva and saliva enzymes.
- Now place the mashed-up food into the plastic bag. The bag represents the stomach. Add some blue food colouring to represent the bile from the liver.
- Now add some vinegar to illustrate the acids and squeeze the bag to show the stomach muscles at work.
- Finally, add some washing-up liquid to represent the enzymes digesting the food.

Variations

- Instead of a banana, you could use another type of food. Discuss how hard we have to work to chew tougher foods.
- Draw the human digestive system and label all the different parts, then do the same with a cow's. How are the systems different and how are they the same?

Challenge questions

- How has the banana changed in appearance and smell?
- Do you think you would be able to recognise all the different foods you eat if you examined the contents of your stomach?

- Which types of food are the easiest to digest, do you think?
- Saliva and gastric juice have special chemicals to help break down food – what they are called?
- Gastric juices contain a very powerful acid – why is this?
- Why is fibre important in our diet?
- Some foods need to be chewed for a longer time than others. Can you name some foods that need to be chewed for a longer time than others and why?
- Why aren't we able to digest foods like corn or lettuce completely?
- Do all animals have the same digestive systems?
- How long does it take to digest food?
- What is the function of saliva?
- Can you think of three reasons why we eat food?
- Can you find out about nutrients and what they are?
- What are proteins used for?
- Can you find out about Lazzaro Spallanzani and the experiments he did?
- How can doctors see inside our stomachs? What is the device they use and who invented it?
- Can you find out what causes heartburn or indigestion?
- Why does your stomach rumble?
- Sometimes your digestive system may produce a rather smelly gas. Can you find out why and what the gas is made of?

Safety consideration

- Care needs to be taken when using the knife to slice up food.

Seed pop

Seed pop is a great experiment for showing how some plants disperse their seeds by explosion.

Theme

Green plants

Suitable for

KS1
KS2

Aim

- To understand about the parts of the flower and their role in the life cycle of flowering plants, including pollination, seed formation, seed dispersal and germination.

Resources

- Balloon
- Paper confetti/paper contents of a hole punch
- Pin

What to do

- Ask children how plants disperse their seeds. Discuss together all the different ways.
- Now tell children that you will show them one method of dispersal using a balloon which acts as a seedcase. Ask them to suggest what could be used for the seeds.
- Fill a balloon with the paper contents of a hole punch or some homemade confetti (use a funnel).
- Now blow up the balloon and tie it.
- Making sure that children are a safe distance away from the balloon, use a pin to pop the balloon.
- The 'seeds' will disperse and scatter everywhere.

- Discuss real-life seed dispersal and how this happens. Some fruits scatter their seeds by literally exploding – the pod dries, bursts open and forcibly shoots the seeds for several feet in all directions. This reduces competition between the parent plant and the seeds. It also reduces overcrowding and it provides opportunities to spread the plant to new localities.

Variations

- Go on a seed-search hike and hunt for seeds in their natural setting. Locate as many seeds as possible and record what has been discovered on an observation chart. Use a microscope to look at the seeds found more closely.
- Look on Google for images (still and moving) of seed dispersal by explosion.
- Replicate the way seeds are dispersed by wind using a fan to blow the seeds about the classroom.
- Ask pupils to create a timeline or cartoon strip of the dispersal process of a single seed from the adult plant to a place where it can grow into a new plant.
- Make a Venn diagram with three interlocking circles labelled: 'wind', 'animals as consumers' and 'animals as carriers'. Cut out pictures of plants and their seeds, then place them in the correct circle for their method of dispersal.

Challenge questions

- How many different methods of seed dispersal are there?
- Can the same seed be spread by more than one method?
- Why do plants disperse their seeds?
- Do you think glitter would work well inside the balloon instead of confetti?
- Can you find out about plants that need heat to open up their seed pods?
- What influences how seeds are dispersed?
- How many types of seed can you think of?
- What factors might decrease the spread of seeds?
- What percentage of seeds that are dispersed by explosion actually germinate?
- Does a pod have to be dry for seeds to be scattered by explosion?
- Which method of seed dispersal do the following plants use: thistle, geranium, dandelion, bramble, burdock, sycamore, flag iris, gorse, hazel, lupin?
- Can you find out about the squirting cucumber using the internet or reference books?

Safety consideration

- Make sure that children are kept well away from the exploding balloon.

Busy bees

Busy bees is a fun activity that demonstrates pollination in the classroom through role play.

Theme

Green plants

Suitable for

KS1
KS2

Aims

- To understand about the parts of the flower and their role in the life cycle of flowering plants, including pollination, seed formation, seed dispersal and germination.
- To understand that insects pollinate some flowers.

Resources

- There are various resources you can use to represent the different parts of a flower and a bee. For example:

sepals and petals	shapes out of card and fixed to clothing or a headband
stamens	a yoghurt pot to act as a holder for the pollen grains
pollen grains	film pot lids; ping pong balls; card discs; Velcro balls (cover ping pong balls with Velcro)
stigma	a woolly hat or balaclava
nectar	drinks cartons with straws
bee	a headband or hat with antennae; a woolly jumper; black and yellow striped trousers; sunglasses; wings made out of wire coat hangers and a pair of nylon tights

- Photos of bees
- Video clip of a bee pollinating a flower

What to do

- Discuss with children why they think bees visit flowers and what they think happens when they do. Look at some photos of bees together.

- Explain that bees are just like flying Velcro patches and that you can demonstrate this through role play.

- Dress children up as the different flower parts and then organise them into groups to form two flowers and a bee. A flower with five sepals, five petals, five stamens and one stigma involves sixteen children.

- Explain the roles that each part of the flower plays – i.e. petals and perfume try to attract the bee and nectar is offered to the bee as food; stamens transfer pollen onto the back of the bee; the stigma transfers pollen from the back of the bee.

- The 'bee' visits the first flower, making buzzing noises. It collects pollen by removing a pollen grain from the pot. It then 'flies' to the second flower, which is waving its petals to attract the bee. The bee deposits the pollen on the stigma by brushing the velcro hooks against the woolly hat.

- This can be repeated several times.

- Discuss pollination in more detail and talk together about any concepts that children seem unsure of. Explain that flowers have evolved a natural form of Velcro on their petals to help insects get a grip, making it easier for them to pay a visit and collect nectar while carrying out that vital job of pollination. Discuss the importance of insects in plant reproduction and that some plants would not be able to reproduce without them.

- Show a video clip from the internet of a bee pollinating a flower or observe some bees on growing flowers from a safe distance.

Variations

- Use a bag of pot pourri or cheap bottles of perfume for scent.
- Demonstrate as part of a school assembly.
- Visit a botanic garden to see different pollinators at work.
- Have students work in pairs to explore Velcro fasteners under a microscope.
- Study the features of cut flowers. Touch one of the flowers lightly with a dry paintbrush and then tap the brush on a piece of paper. This shows how it has picked up the pollen.

Challenge questions

- Which plants do bees seem to like best?
- How can bees tell the difference between rough and smooth petals?
- Where on their bodies do bees gather pollen?
- What is the long hollow tube that bees use to collect nectar?
- What do you think would happen if the bee population was dramatically reduced or if bees became extinct?
- Can you find out who invented Velcro?
- How does the structure of Velcro relate to its function?

Flower power

> Flower power is a fun activity to illustrate how insects help with the cross-pollination of plants.

Theme

Green plants

Suitable for

KS1
KS2

Aims

- To understand about the parts of the flower and their role in the life cycle of flowering plants, including pollination, seed formation, seed dispersal and germination.
- To understand that insects pollinate some flowers.

Resources

- Two margarine tubs, one containing red powder paint and the other white
- Two collecting dishes
- Cotton buds

What to do

- You can choose to do this activity in a large hall or outdoors.
- Divide the class into two teams and arrange them in lines at one end of your chosen space.
- At the other end of the space, two tubs should be placed on the ground, one with red powder and the other with white powder. These represent the stamens producing the pollen for two different flowers.

- All team members act as bees. The first member of each team runs to the first tub carrying a cotton bud and collects some 'pollen'. The team member returns to their team and deposits the pollen in a dish. The child repeats this activity for the second tub of differently coloured pollen.
- The remaining team members take turns until they have all completed the activity.
- In doing this, children are mixing up the 'pollen', showing how cross-pollination takes place.

Variations

- Turn this into a competition to see how much pollen can be collected in five minutes.
- Use a third tub of coloured paint.

Challenge questions

- What time of the day is best to collect pollen?
- Do you think that bees drop pollen as they move from place to place?
- Do all bees carry pollen?
- What do bees do with the honey and pollen they collect?
- What happens to a bee if it cannot find any pollen?
- Can you find out about waggle dances and how bees talk to each other?
- How much of what we eat comes from insect-pollinated plants?
- What other insects act as pollinators?

My space

> My space is a whole-body activity to illustrate the relationship between people and their environment.

Theme

Living things in their environment

Suitable for

KS1
KS2

Aims

- To understand about the ways in which living things and the environment need protection.
- To understand that different plants and animals are found in different habitats.
- To introduce the concept of woodland habitats.

Resources

- Chairs
- CD player

What to do

- This activity is best suited to a large indoor hall or an outside space.
- Each child takes a chair from the classroom into the activity area and sits in a space away from everyone else. Explain to children that the chairs represent trees and they themselves are woodland creatures.
- Explain to children that they are going to play a game of musical chairs and that when the music stops they, as woodland creatures, have to find a place to live, i.e. find a chair to sit on.

- Tell children that you will play some music and remove one or two chairs at a time. Ask what might have happened to the trees that are no longer there. For example, they may have been cut down for timber or to make room for a housing development, or damaged by a storm or by grazing.
- After the game, discuss what it felt like to be without a chair. Children will realise that when the tree is removed, the home of the woodland creatures is destroyed and they therefore have to find somewhere else to live.

Variations

- Children can wear masks or labels to represent different creatures.
- Put a pretend road through the chairs (use rope across the activity area) to separate the game into two. Creatures cannot cross from one side to the other. Children will soon realise the dangers that habitat destruction entails when you remove more chairs from one side and none or only a few from the other and the creatures are forced to try to cross the road.
- Explore a specific woodland habitat, the organisms that live there and how they survive.

Challenge questions

- Why is it important to plant more trees?
- Why might it be important to chop down trees?
- Why might climate change be a good thing for trees in Britain?
- Why is tree pruning necessary? Does this destroy habitats?
- Can you find out more about the ancient Caledonian forest in Scotland and how much of it there is now left?

Safety consideration

- Establish some ground rules for playing habitat musical chairs safely.

Gotcha!

Gotcha! is a participatory activity to illustrate the relationship between predator and prey.

Theme

Living things in their environment

Suitable for

KS1
KS2

Aims

- To understand that food chains show feeding relationships in a habitat.
- To learn in a participatory activity about the importance of sight and hearing senses for the survival of both prey and predator.

Resources

- Blindfolds for the predator and prey

What to do

- Introduce the prey/predator relationship by asking children what they already know about the predator and prey relationship. Make a list of all the predators and prey they know of.
- Ask children what skills they think a predator might need to be successful in a hunt and what skills a prey may need to avoid capture. Elicit how children think prey avoids capture and how predators avoid being seen/heard.
- Now select a large activity area, either inside or outside.
- Ask children to sit in a circle and choose two to be the predator and the prey.

- The two children selected stand in the centre of the circle and are blindfolded. The predator should try to pursue the prey while the prey tries to elude the predator. The prey and predator should use their hearing to elude and pursue. This is a version of tag but with blindfolds.

- The rest of the class observe in silence, looking at what senses the predator relied upon to capture the prey: what were some of the things both the prey and the predator had to do to be successful?

- Everyone can have a turn at being either the predator or the prey.

Variations

- Blindfold the prey, but not the predator and vice versa.
- This game can also be played in the style of tag rugby.
- More realism can be injected by the use of animal masks.

Challenge questions

- What would happen if the environment were affected by a chance event, such as a tornado, hurricane or severe drought? Would predators or prey be more likely to survive?
- Are predators to be judged as successful or not based only on the number of prey they consume, or are there other factors that need to be considered?
- Is there safety in numbers for prey? Are you more likely to survive as a prey than a predator if you live in a large population?
- Do populations of predator and prey change over time?
- Can you think of three reasons for the population of a prey species to increase?
- Can you think of three reasons for the population of a predator species to increase?
- Can you think of three reasons for the population of a prey species to decrease?
- Can you think of three reasons for the population of a predator species to decrease?
- How successful might *you* be if you lived in the wild? What would you need to do in order to survive?

Safety consideration

- Care should be taken when playing this game and ground rules need to be established concerning running and contact.

Straw heart

Straw heart is an excellent activity for showing how the heart acts as a powerful muscle pumping blood through the body.

Theme

Humans and other animals

Suitable for

KS1
KS2

Aim

- To understand that the heart acts as a pump to circulate the blood through the vessels around the body, including through the lungs.

Resources

- Drinking straws
- Plasticine

What to do

- This activity should be done first as a demonstration.
- Poke a straw into a lump of plasticine. Now lie on your back and find the pulse in your neck. Put two fingers on the side of your neck, near the front, and move them around until you can feel something thumping under your skin.
- Lay the putty on top of this spot so that the tip of the straw is just above your eyes.
- Now watch what happens as the straw moves in time with your beating heart and you can see your pulse right before your eyes.

- To get your pulse rate, count how many times the straw moves in one minute. To save time, you can also count the number of times the straw moves in 15 seconds and then multiply that by four. Children should now try the activity for themselves.

- Discuss with children what is happening: every heartbeat creates a wave of pressure as blood flows along the arteries. Where these arteries lie close to the surface, this pressure wave can be felt as a pulse. Each contraction sends a pressure wave through your arteries, which causes the straw to vibrate like a metronome.

Variations

- You can also find your pulse in your arm, temples and ankles.
- Come up with different activities that you think might change your pulse rate and keep a table of results.

Challenge questions

- Do you think your pulse rate is always the same?
- Could you do something to change it?
- Is heart beat the same as pulse?
- What is the radial pulse?
- Why should you not use your thumb to take someone else's pulse?
- What is a pulse in music terms?

Safety consideration

- Children with medical problems should not be put at risk when investigating the effect of exercise on heart rate. See www.bhf.org.uk for further information.

Catch me if you can

Catch me if you can is a quick-fire and enjoyable experiment for testing reaction times.

Theme

Keeping healthy

Suitable for

KS1
KS2

Aim

● To test the fingertip reaction times of children.

Resource

● 30 cm rulers

Cyncoed Learning Centre
Cardiff Metropolitan University
Cyncoed Road

What to do

● Explain to children that reaction time is the ability to respond quickly to a stimulus. It is important in many jobs, sports and day-to-day activities, though it is not often measured. For example, to be a fighter pilot you need very fast reactions – when travelling at speeds of over 700 mph, every split second can make all the difference.

● One child holds the ruler near the 30 cm mark and lets it hang vertically. Another child places their thumb and index finger either side of the 0 cm mark and stands ready to catch it when it falls – their fingers shouldn't touch the ruler.

● Without warning, the child holding the ruler lets go and the other tries to catch the ruler as quickly as possible.

- Record the level (in cm) where the second child caught the ruler. The shorter the time, the faster the child's reactions.
- The same person is tested five times and the mean average of their results is calculated (add all five numbers together and then divide by five).
- Now the pairs should swap over so that the first child is tested.
- Explain that the experiment tests how long it takes the brain to translate visual information into voluntary motor commands and actions.
- Look at the table below. The 'mean catch distance' on the ruler can be converted into a 'mean reaction time' in milliseconds.

Distance/reaction time conversion table:

Catch distance (cm)	Reaction time (milliseconds)	Catch distance (cm)	Reaction time (milliseconds)
1	50	16	180
2	60	17	190
3	70	18	190
4	80	19	200
5	90	20	200
6	100	21	210
7	120	22	210
8	130	23	220
9	140	24	220
10	140	25	230
11	150	26	230
12	160	27	230
13	160	28	240
14	170	29	240
15	170	30	250

Reaction time (milliseconds)	Rating	Comment
0–50	Out of this world	What planet are you from?
50–130	Outstanding	Computer game addict by any chance?
131–175	Excellent	You're a frequent text messager, aren't you?
176–200	Good	It's good but not that good.
201–240	Average	Not bad but not good.
241–250	Fair	Has it been a long day?
251+	Slow	Open your eyes next time.

Variations

- Repeat the experiment by altering the way children stand.
- The first child should warn their partner with a countdown of three when they will release the ruler.

Challenge questions

- When do you think reaction times might be useful in real life?
- Do you think reaction times vary for people of different ages?
- Do you think reaction times vary for people who are tired?
- Do you think reaction times vary for men and women?
- Do you think reaction times vary depending on your mood?
- Do you think reaction times vary after an alcoholic drink?
- Can you complete the following? If a millisecond is one thousandth of a second, then this means that:

    One second (s) = _____milliseconds (ms)
    Half of a second (0.5s) = _____ ms
    A quarter of a second (0.25s) = _____ ms
    One tenth of a second (0.1s) = _____ ms

Chapter 4
Materials and their properties - experiments

'When you smell an odourless gas, it is probably carbon monoxide.'

Sink or swim

Sink or swim is an enquiry-based activity to develop children's understanding of sinking and floating. This investigation acts as a precursor to further exploration of density of solids and liquids.

Theme

Scientific enquiry

Suitable for

KS1
KS2

Aim

- To encourage skills in experimental design, testing simple hypotheses, and grouping objects by common characteristics.

Resources

- Various objects for testing made of a variety of materials, selected by you and the children, such as wood, metal, plastic and paper. Possibilities include: paperclips, soap, toothpicks, bottle caps, marbles, plastic beads and cubes, sponge pieces, pencils, pieces of aluminium foil and paper, golf balls, ping pong balls, apples, rubbers, Styrofoam packing peanuts and so on.
- Buckets or bowls
- Water
- Pan balance or electronic balance
- Old newspapers

What to do

- Cover tables in newspaper and give children a collection of objects.
- Children discuss in groups of three characteristics by which the objects could be classified (for example, colour, weight, size, shape, composition, bendability and so on).

- Children then share their classification scheme with the class and share ideas.

- Discuss the different ways that children separated their pile of materials and point out that different objects can be described by a number of characteristics, including the type of material from which they are made, their size, their shape, their colour and their weight. Some objects can be characterised by their purpose: for example, buttons and paperclips are both designed to hold things together.

- Follow this by discussing another characteristic that children may not have considered – whether the objects will float or sink in water.

- As a class, generate a list of descriptive words for objects that float and one for objects that sink.

- Look at two objects to start the activity, a paperclip and an apple. Ask which will float and which will sink.

- Children may predict that, because the apple is heavier, it should sink. Demonstrate that the apple floats and the paperclip sinks.

- Point out that there is more to floating and sinking than just weight. Tell children that they will be exploring this idea further by using and adding to the activity sheet below:

Object	Prediction: we think it will ... sink or float	What it did	Was the prediction correct?	Notes
Apple	sink	float	no	This is heavier than a paperclip so why did it float?
Paperclip	float	sink	no	The paperclip is light so it should have floated?
Golf ball				
Ping pong ball				
2p coin				
Toothpick				

Object	Prediction: we think it will ... sink or float	What it did	Was the prediction correct?	Notes
Sponge				
Marble				
Egg				
Soap				

- Children will now collect together some more objects of their own choice to test their predictions (hypotheses) and record their data.

- After objects have been tested, groups should confer to decide whether any items should be re-tested. Some items may seem to float, then sink as they become wet. Others may have densities similar to water and may float in the middle of the bucket rather than on top of the water.

- Children present their findings to the class as a poster or an oral presentation. They should reveal the items that did and did not float, and describe what conclusions they drew about what types of item do and do not float in water.

- Lead a discussion about how we describe objects that float or sink. Refer back to the words children originally used to describe items that float or sink. Ask children to look for commonalities among the items that float and those that sink. Which descriptive words would they change? Are there words they would add?

- Introduce new vocabulary. For example, objects that float can be described as buoyant. The concept of density can also be introduced at this time; a good visual demonstration is the buoyancy of a golf ball and a ping pong ball. They have similar volumes but one is much heavier and therefore more dense.

Variation

- Children can hypothesise whether the type of liquid makes a difference in this experiment. They can explore hot versus cold water, salt water, soapy water, vegetable oil or baby oil.

Challenge questions

- How full will your bucket be for each object tested? Do you need a certain amount of water to be able to test fairly whether something floats? Should it be the same amount of water for each item?
- How will you place the object in the bucket? Will you drop it in? If so, from what height? Will you place it halfway down into the water and then let it go? Will you place it on the bottom of the bucket and then let it go? Will you put the object in the bucket and then add water?
- How will you define floating? Is anything that is not on the bottom floating? Does the item have to rise all the way to the top of the water?

Safety consideration

- Care should be taken using containers of water and tables should be covered in newspaper to protect them.

Invisible ink

Invisible ink is an exciting experiment to show how a weak acid can be used to weaken paper and write secret, invisible messages.

Theme

Characteristics of materials

Suitable for

KS1
KS2

Aims

- To compare everyday materials and objects on the basis of their material properties.
- To describe changes that occur when materials are heated or cooled.

Resources

- Lemons or lemon juice
- Heat source: for example, candle, sunlight, light bulb
- Paper
- Paintbrush or stick

What to do

- Tell children that they are going to write a secret message using invisible ink. Discuss whether there is such a thing. Who might use it?
- Squeeze some lemons to obtain their juice, or use bottled lemon juice.
- Now ask for a volunteer to write a message on paper, using the lemon juice as ink. Use a fine paintbrush to write with.
- Let the paper dry.

- Hold the paper up to the class – can they see what is written? Be careful not to hold it up to the light (perhaps place a book behind it).
- Now hold the paper up to sunlight, a light bulb or other heat source.
- The heat will cause the writing to darken to a pale brown, so the message can now be read.
- Give each child some paper, a paintbrush and lemon juice for them to write their own secret message.

Variations

- Another way to read the message is to put salt on the drying ink. After a minute, wipe the salt off and colour over the paper with a wax crayon to reveal the message.
- Experiment with other liquids, such as apple juice, orange juice, onion juice, vinegar, cola, honey solution, sugar solution, milk or soap water.
- Try heating your paper using a radiator to reveal the hidden message.

Challenge questions

- Can you find out whether valuable objects in your school, such as computers, have been property-marked – what substance has been used and how can the marks be made visible?
- Why is it important that an ideal invisible ink should be odourless?
- Can you find out about other invisible ink types, such as inks developed by chemical reaction?
- Why is invisible ink relevant to national security?

Safety consideration

- Be careful not to overdo the heating of the paper.

Messy mixtures

Messy mixtures tests children's knowledge and understanding of sorting mixtures. This is a practical hands-on activity that children will enjoy doing together.

Theme

Separating mixtures of materials

Suitable for

KS1
KS2

Aims

- To use knowledge of solids, liquids and gases to decide how mixtures might be separated.
- To use appropriate scientific language and terms.

Resources

- Mixed beans and paperclips
- Mixed flour and rice
- Mixed tea leaves and coffee
- Mixed flour, lentils, rice and beans
- Mixed tea leaves and sand
- Different sizes of sieve
- Magnet
- Filter paper
- Funnel
- Tea strainer
- Colander
- Cotton wool
- Water

What to do

- Tell children that there was an Earth tremor last night that shook the house. Explain that when you went into the kitchen, all of the contents of one of your cupboards had spilled onto the floor. Rather than sweep up and throw everything away, you decided to sort the mess by separating all the things on the floor.

- Tell children what you found mixed together: beans and paperclips; flour and rice; tea leaves and coffee; flour, lentils, rice and beans; tea leaves and sand.

- Organise children into small groups of three or four and ask them to discuss how they would separate the messy mixtures.

- After a period of discussion, children can have a go at testing out their ideas. Distribute the messy mixtures to each group and have all equipment close at hand for children to select.

- Supervise children's attempts to separate the mixtures and call a pit stop to the lesson to offer ideas, prompts and challenges.

- After a time, draw the class together and talk about the separation techniques used. Which ones were successful? Which were appropriate? Which were inappropriate?

- Demonstrate the separation techniques at the end of the lesson, discussing each one in turn.

Variations

- Organise groups differently so that one group is responsible for magnet separation only, another group responsible for sieve separation, and so on.
- Think about what other materials from the kitchen cupboard could be combined.

Challenge questions

- Could some mixtures be separated using more than one method?
- Were some methods more difficult and time consuming than others?
- How could you prevent materials from becoming mixed together in the first place?

Safety considerations

- Ensure that all equipment is clean to start with so that mixtures are not contaminated.
- Children should wash their hands after the experiment.

Soft, strong and very long

Soft, strong and very long tests the claims of a toilet paper manufacturer against other brands.

Theme

Grouping and classifying materials

Suitable for

KS1
KS2

Aims

- To compare and contrast materials.
- To conduct a fair test.
- To make systematic observations and measurements.

Resources

- YouTube clip of Andrex advert
- Four different brands of toilet tissue
- Water
- Microscopes
- Bulldog clips
- Forcemeters

What to do

- If possible, show the class the TV advertisement for Andrex toilet tissue.
- Focus on the claim that Andrex toilet paper is 'soft, strong and very long'. Ask the class to think of ways they could test the claim.
- Organise children into small groups and allow them some time to discuss ideas.

- As a class, share the discussions and decide how to conduct a fair scientific test to investigate the Andrex claim.
- Decide what will be tested: for example, length and thickness, absorbency, strength and softness.
- Before investigating the absorbency, give children some microscopes so they can examine the brands and make a prediction.
- Let children investigate using their own ideas. Help children to develop certain tests if they need support: for example, to test strength, use a bulldog clip to hold ten sheets of toilet paper at one end and use a forcemeter to pull the other end.
- After all the tests have been conducted, share the results and the comparisons made. Are the Andrex claims fair?

Variations

- You could try this experiment using other products, such as kitchen paper.
- Look carefully at the claims made by various manufacturers. Invent your own advertising claim for one of the other brands.
- Present the results of this investigation as a poster and display it in class.

Challenge questions

- How did you ensure that the investigation was fair? Were the tissues single-ply?
- How do the toilet tissues compare for value? Is it better to buy more of the cheaper brands? What do the unit values work out as?
- Can you think of ten other uses for toilet tissue?

Safety consideration

- Ensure that all toilet tissue is fresh from the packet and not from the bathroom.

Attractive pennies

Attractive pennies is an interesting activity that tests the magnetic properties of an assortment of 1p and 2p coins.

Theme

Grouping and classifying materials, forces and motion

Suitable for

KS1
KS2

Aims

- To compare and contrast materials.
- To conduct a fair test.
- To make systematic observations and measurements.

Resources

- Assorted new 1p and 2p (post-1992) coins made of steel (these are magnetic) and some older 1p and 2p (pre-1993) coins made of bronze (not magnetic)
- Assorted magnets, including a rare-earth neodymium magnet

What to do

- Distribute a variety of magnets per group.
- Give pupils a selection of older and newer 2p and 1p coins. Ask them to test for magnetism and try to come up with a solution as to why some are magnetic and some not.

- Ask children what they notice about the pennies that are and are not attracted to the magnet (for example, dates and shininess). Newer coins are likely to be shinier or less worn. Some pupils may not be aware that coins are dated, so will need to be prompted to examine the coins closely.
- Challenge children to use what they have found out to predict if a particular coin will be magnetic or not.
- Can they separate the coins into metal types and name them?
- Children should use the internet to find out more.
- Explain that 'copper' (1p and 2p) coins produced after 1992 are made from copper-plated steel (earlier coins were made from bronze). Steel is an alloy of iron and carbon; it's the iron that makes the coins magnetic. Iron, nickel and cobalt are the only magnetic metals.
- Challenge children to balance coins one on top of the other using magnetism.

Variation

- Repeat this experiment with 5p, 10p, 20p, 50p, £1 and £2 coins.

Challenge questions

- How many pennies can you attract to a magnet?
- Can you suspend a string of pennies on your magnet?
- Which is the best magnet for suspending a string of pennies?
- What is the most unusual shape you can make with the pennies and magnet?
- Can you make a penny spin without touching it?
- Do pennies need to be made of metal?
- What magnetic penny tricks can you do?

Safety consideration

- Tell children to be careful when bringing two rare-earth magnets together because there is a danger of getting skin trapped between them.

A sticky situation

A sticky situation is a hands-on experiment for making glue.

Theme

Changing materials

Suitable for

KS1
KS2

Aims

- To compare and contrast materials.
- To describe changes that occur when materials are mixed.

Resources

- Skimmed milk
- Baking soda
- Vinegar
- Measuring cup
- Measuring spoons
- Paper towels
- Rubber bands
- Aprons

What to do

- Tell children that the school has run out of glue and so they have to make their own.
- Ask children what they think glue is made of. They may have made glue from flour and water before. Tell them that this time you will demonstrate how to make glue from vinegar and milk.
- Add two tablespoons of vinegar to half a cup of skimmed milk. Stir them together and let the mixture sit for a couple of minutes.

- Ask children if they have heard of curds and whey. Explain that the vinegar will make the protein in the milk stick together to form small white lumps called curds. The leftover liquid is called whey.
- Explain that the curds can be strained as whey is not needed to make glue. Ask children how this might be done.
- Explain that a strainer can be made by putting a folded paper towel over an empty cup and attaching it with a rubber band.
- Pour the curds and whey into the cup with the paper towel. The whey will go through the paper towel and the curds will stay on top. Wait a few minutes for the whey to drain through the paper towel.
- Now use a spoon to remove the curds carefully and put them between two dry paper towels. Press down to get all the whey out.
- Next put the curds into another cup, stir in two teaspoons of water and then add one teaspoon of baking soda. Explain that the baking soda reacts with the vinegar that is in the curds, producing carbon dioxide. Add some more water if the mixture is not glue-like.
- Next try sticking some materials together to form a collage using the newly formed glue.
- Now set children off to make glue themselves. They should wear aprons to protect their clothes.

Variations

- Try making glue using flour and water instead.
- Try using different types of milk other than skimmed.
- Try using different types of vinegar.

Challenge questions

- Instead of vinegar, what else could you use?
- How would you make the glue stronger?
- Will the glue be more suitable for sticking together particular materials?
- What other recipes and methods can you think of to make your own homemade glue?

Safety consideration

- This is a potentially sticky lesson and children should be careful what they touch. They should wash their hands thoroughly after the experiment.

Dirty money

> Dirty money is a brilliant activity for showing children how acid can be used to clean tarnished coins.

Theme

Changing materials

Suitable for

KS1
KS2

Aims

- To compare and contrast materials.
- To describe changes that occur when materials are mixed.

Resources

- A collection of tarnished 1p and 2p coins
- Vinegar
- Salt water
- Baking soda mixed with water
- Lemon juice
- Cola
- Water
- Soapy water
- Milk
- Small cups
- Spoons
- Pencil and paper

What to do

- Explain to children that you have a number of 1p and 2p coins that are dirty and that you'd like to clean them but are not sure how. Can they help?
- Take ideas from children and discuss together.
- Say that you have some different solutions given to you by different friends who all say that their solution will work best. Explain that it is the children's job to test each one.
- Before starting, ask children to make a hypothesis and predict which solutions they think will work best. The solutions are: vinegar, salt water, baking soda and water, lemon juice, cola, water, soapy water and milk.
- Start children off by showing them what to do. For example, pour some milk into a cup containing a dirty 1p coin. Stir the cup and leave for ten minutes.
- While you are waiting, explain the importance of conducting a fair test. Discuss the variables they will need to consider and draw up a planning board together.
- Take the penny out of the milk and dry it. What has happened?
- Now ask children to compare this result with the result they get from the other solutions.
- At the end of the testing period, see which solutions were the best at cleaning. The pennies should be cleaned best by the strongest acid – the lemon juice.
- Explain that acids are better penny cleaners. Tell children that if you were to leave a penny in vinegar or lemon juice for several days, small pieces of the penny would eventually start to come off!

Variations

- Instead of leaving the pennies for ten minutes, rub the pennies with each solution the same number of times.
- Try mixing salt with each of the solutions and see what happens.
- Use different types of lemon juice from different retailers – this should produce varying results.

Challenge questions

- Was this experiment difficult to do fairly?
- What other solutions could you test?
- Were you really cleaning the pennies or dissolving the tarnish?
- If you did this experiment with five different types of lemon juice, why might there be differences in the results? For example, the strength of juices might vary by season. Does it matter in which country the lemons were grown? Does the ripeness make a difference?
- Can you name some common household acids?
- Can you name an acid found in your body?
- Do you think milk contains acid?
- Does cleaning old coins with lemon juice devalue the coins?
- Try to find out about pH – what does it mean?

Safety consideration

- All solutions coming into contact with hands will need to be washed off thoroughly.

It's a buzz

> It's a buzz tests salt water and other solutions for electrical conductivity.

Theme

Grouping and classifying materials

Suitable for

KS1
KS2

Aims

- To compare and contrast materials.
- To show that some materials are better electrical conductors than others.

Resources

- Buzzer
- Two art/craft sticks
- Tin foil
- Battery
- Masking tape
- Cup
- Salt water
- Other solutions you would like to test

What to do

- Take two small art/craft sticks and cover them with tin foil.
- Take the red wire of a buzzer and attach it with masking tape to the positive end of a battery.

- Take the black wire of the buzzer and attach it with masking tape to one of the foil-covered craft sticks. Make sure it is securely taped down. If the wire pulls away from the stick, the experiment will not work.
- Take the remaining craft stick and tape it to the negative end of the battery.
- Gently touch the two craft sticks together. If you've made your tester properly, you'll hear a buzz.
- Dip the two ends of your tester into a cup of salt water. Leave a small gap between the sticks of one to two inches. If the buzzer buzzes, you are conducting electricity.
- Test other liquids, such as tap water, cola, etc.
- Explain the science at work here: the buzzer buzzes in salt water because the salt water acts like an invisible wire to connect the circuit. When you add salt to water, the salt molecules dissolve in the water and break into smaller parts called ions. The ions carry electricity through the water.

Variations

- You could test different types of fizzy drinks to see whether they conduct electricity.
- Instead of a buzzer, can you make a light bulb light up?

Challenge questions

- If you add more salt to your water, what happens to the buzz? Does it get louder?
- Does tap water contain sodium?
- Does fresh water contain sodium?
- Will the temperature of the water make a difference to its electrical conductivity?

Safety consideration

- Point out that a larger battery would present safety issues and that there could be a risk of electrocution.

Handle with care

> Handle with care is an experiment to show how hard an eggshell really is.

Theme

Grouping and classifying materials

Suitable for

KS1
KS2

Aim

- To compare everyday materials and objects on the basis of their properties.

Resources

- Eggs
- Bottle caps
- Newspaper
- Wooden or plastic chopping board
- Weights

What to do

- Although eggs can break easily, they are also very strong (but only in one direction). Discuss with children why eggshells need to be strong: for example, to stop the growing chick from being squashed by the adult bird. The shell also protects the chick from infection, but allows it to get oxygen and get rid of carbon dioxide.

- Ask children to think how many books four eggs could support.

- Explain the experiment – cover a table with newspaper and then put four bottle caps on the table and balance whole eggs (raw or hard-boiled), small end down, in the bottle caps.

- Carefully put a wooden board on top of the eggs and then place weights on top until the eggs break.
- Explain that the dome end of an egg is much stronger than its side. Domes distribute the weight at the top to all parts of the eggshell. Bridge arches work in a similar way. A dome essentially distributes the weight and the pressure applied on the top evenly to the entire structure. In architecture, the dome is one of the strongest designs because it supports the weight of the roof evenly, so that no single point on the dome supports the whole load and gives way under stress. Similarly, the dome shape of each end of the egg distributes all the weight evenly and minimises stress and strain.

Variations

- Repeat the experiment with the eggs balanced on their side. Do they support the same amount of weight?
- To avoid making a mess, use a bottle cut in half, invert the top into the base to make a funnel and cover with a piece of circular card. Place the egg into the inverted neck of the bottle, so that when it breaks its contents run down into the bottle.

Challenge questions

- Do all types of egg share the same shape?
- Are some eggs stronger than others? For example, compare an ostrich egg with a hen's egg.
- If you squeeze the ends of an egg between the palms of your hands, do you think it will break?
- Why do you think that eggs are sold in markets and supermarkets with their ends pointing up? Are there good reasons for not storing them horizontally?
- Look at a picture of the Taj Mahal or a mosque. What do you notice about the roof?
  Why is it designed in this shape?
- Could eggs support the weight of someone in your class?

Safety considerations

- Make sure that the eggs are cleaned thoroughly before use, or handle them using plastic gloves.
- Dispose of broken eggs safely. Children should not touch raw egg and should wear plastic gloves to clear away.

Bungee jump

Bungee jump is an exciting experiment in which children design a bungee jump to save an egg. The activity provides an excellent context for children to explore concepts of force and motion, and energy transformations.

Theme

Grouping and classifying materials

Suitable for

KS1
KS2

Aim

- To compare everyday materials and objects on the basis of their material properties.

Resources

- Eggs
- Pennies
- Tights
- Masking tape
- Ruler
- Scissors
- Newspaper

What to do

- Cover the area with newspaper and tell children that their challenge is to design a bungee jump ride for an egg.
- The rules are that the egg cannot break or hit the ground and the bungee must come within 7 cm of the floor, without touching the floor.

- Give children the materials they will need. Ask them to think about how stretchy the tights are and how long the bungee cord needs to be. Can children think what the pennies might be used for? For example, as a test.

- They should use tape to attach a bungee cord to a launch site and test the jump.

- Children should measure how close the test egg (penny) comes to the ground and make any necessary adjustments.

- When all changes have been made, children can use real eggs to test their bungee group by group.

- A scoring method can be devised such as the following, and the team with the most points declared the winners:

    The jump is within 5 cm of the ground
    The jump is 5 to 10 cm from the ground
    The jump is 10 to 20 cm from the ground
    The jump is 20 to 30 cm from the ground
    The jump is 30 to 40 cm from the ground
    The jump is more than 40 cm from the ground

- Now spend time together discussing and explaining the experiment as a class. When the egg is dropped, the egg stretches the bungee cord. As the cord stretches, it slows the egg until it stops falling. Then the bungee cord springs back, pulling the egg up and away from the ground. The bungee cord stretches because it is made from materials that are elastic. Things that are elastic return almost to their original shape after they have been stretched or squashed by a force. The amount the bungee cord stretches depends on how elastic the materials are and how much the egg weighs.

Variations

- You could use a golf ball instead of an egg.
- Use rubber bands instead of tights for the bungee. Loop some rubber bands together to make a cord. A washing machine mesh bag could be used for the harness.
- Record a series of bungee jumps using a force sensor.

Challenge questions

- What would happen if you used different tights? For example, do they all have the same elasticity?
- If you keep on using the same tights to try out your bungee jump, will the elastic become fatigued?
- What happens if you change the length of the bungee cord?
- What happens if you change how you arrange the materials?
- Does it make a difference if the same person is testing each time?

Safety considerations

- Make sure that the eggs are cleaned thoroughly before use, or handle them using plastic gloves.
- Dispose of broken eggs safely. Children should not touch raw egg, and should wear plastic gloves to clear away.

Hi!

Hi! is a deceptively simple experiment for exploring the reaction of two materials and the effect they have on each other.

Theme

Changing materials

Suitable for

KS1
KS2

Aim

- To observe that non-reversible changes result in the formation of new materials.

Resources

- Vinegar
- Bicarbonate of soda
- Empty bottle
- Balloon
- Rubber bands
- Funnel

What to do

- Pour about an inch of vinegar into an empty bottle.
- Use a funnel to fill a balloon half full of bicarbonate of soda.
- Stretch the open end of the balloon over the neck of the bottle, making sure it is on securely. Tie it with a rubber band. Let the heavy end of the balloon dangle down, so no bicarbonate of soda goes in the bottle.

- Hold onto the balloon at the bottle neck, and pick up the heavy part of the balloon so that all the baking soda falls into the vinegar at the bottom of the bottle.
- Shake the bottle. Now watch what happens!
- Discuss as a class the chemical reaction that has just taken place: when the vinegar and bicarbonate of soda come in contact, a gas called carbon dioxide is released. When this happens, bubbles form and pressure builds, because the density of carbon dioxide is much less than the density of the baking soda or vinegar. The gas tries to escape but has nowhere to go except inside the balloon, which it inflates.

Variations

- Experiment with different amounts of baking soda and vinegar for maximum inflation.
- Try the experiment with differently shaped and sized balloons.
- Instead of balloons, you could use rubber gloves.
- You can do this experiment with plastic ziploc® bags and make a bag explode.

Challenge questions

- Would this experiment work with cola and bicarbonate of soda?
- Would the experiment work if you didn't shake the bottle?
- By what other names is bicarbonate of soda also known?
- How many uses can you find for bicarbonate of soda?

Safety considerations

- There is the possibility that the balloon or rubber glove could fly off if not held down securely with an elastic band.
- Be careful that children do not inhale the bicarbonate of soda or rub it in their eyes.

One potato, two potato

One potato, two potato has nothing to do with potatoes, but with the density of liquids and how they separate when mixed together.

Theme

Separating mixtures of materials

Suitable for

KS1
KS2

Aims

- To understand that all matter in our world can be categorised as solid, liquid or gas.
- To understand that different liquids can have different densities.
- To recognise that the molecules are more compact in some substances than others.

Resources

- Cooking oil
- Syrup
- Water
- Measuring cylinder

What to do

- Show children three different liquids: water, oil and syrup. Have they ever looked closely at oil or syrup before?
- Say that you are going to pour the liquids together into a container – ask children whether they think the liquids will mix or not.

- Now pour equal amounts of oil, water and syrup into a measuring cylinder. Ask why it is important to pour an equal measure of all three.
- Stir the liquids together, or shake the container, and observe what happens as you leave it to stand. The three liquids sit on top of each other and form layers – one potato, two potato, three potato!
- Discuss why three layers are formed. The syrup lies at the bottom, the water in the middle and the oil on top. This is because each liquid has its own density and the liquids are now ordered from highest to lowest density. The oil stays on top because it is least dense.

Variation

- Drop some solids into the solution. Try dropping a penny, a Lego brick, a grain of rice, a grape and a piece of wood chip. What happens? (An object will sink in liquids until it reaches a liquid that has a density greater than itself. Another way to think of this is that lighter objects will sit on top of heavier objects. Which object has the highest density? Which object has the lowest density?)

Challenge questions

- What would happen if you poured the liquids into the measuring container in a different order?
- Have you seen examples of liquid density differences in the real world? Perhaps you have noticed oil or other liquids in water puddles on the ground, or maybe in salad dressing.
- What is the relationship between the experiment above and an oil spill? What do you think happens to the oil that has spilled out of a ship and into the ocean? How might an oil spill be cleaned up?
- Can you find out what a hydrometer is and what it does?
- Can you make your own hydrometer using a drinking straw, two small nails and some Blu-tack?

Let's rock

Let's rock challenges children's ideas about the properties of rocks and stones.

Theme

Grouping and classifying materials

Suitable for

KS1
KS2

Aim

- To describe and group rocks and soils on the basis of their characteristics, including appearance, texture and permeability.

Resources

- A collection of stones and pebbles
- Pumice stone
- Bowl of water

What to do

- Ask children to think about whether rocks can float or not. Discuss as a whole class the properties of rocks.
- Take some stones and pebbles that you have collected and drop them into a bowl of water. What happens?
- Now take a piece of pumice and ask children what they notice about this type of rock that is different from the stones and pebbles.
- Drop the pumice into a bowl of water and see what happens.
- Talk together about why the pumice floats and the other stones and rocks did not.

- Explain the science involved: most rocks are denser than water, with the exception of pumice. Pumice is a volcanic rock and has a considerable amount of gas whipped into it while it is still molten. Upon hardening, the gas bubbles become millions of tiny pockets filled with air. If a specimen has enough of the pockets so that its bulk density is less than that of water, it will float. Pumice is actually a kind of glass and not a mixture of minerals.
- Tell children that floating islands of pumice miles wide have been discovered in the Pacific, some with plants actually growing on them.

Variations

- Repeat the experiment with a larger volume of water.
- Repeat the experiment with different types of water.

Challenge questions

- Is pumice the only rock that will float in water?
- Can you make a pumice stone sink?
- Will a large piece of pumice float or sink?
- How big does a rock have to be to be called a rock?
- Can a rock that would normally sink in tap water float in salt water?
- What are pumice stones used for in the home?
- Would pumice stones make good lifebuoys?
- Where in the world are you likely to find pumice?
- Can you explain why pumice might be found on a beach hundreds of miles from volcanic activity?
- Is pumice a type of foam?

A load of hot air

> **A load of hot air demonstrates how hot air rises using a simple but effective experiment.**

Theme

Grouping and classifying materials

Suitable for

KS1
KS2

Aim

- To describe changes that occur when materials are heated or cooled.

Resources

- Two balloons
- Two jars with wide mouths
- Two skinny bottles with narrow mouths (they need to fit inside the jars)
- Some hot water
- Some iced water

What to do

- Pour hot water into one jar, and pour cold water into the other jar. Fill them both half way.

- Put a balloon over the mouth of a narrow bottle and place the bottle into the jar of hot water. Observe what happens.

- Now put another balloon over the mouth of the other bottle. Place the bottle into the jar of cold water for a few moments, and wait for the result.

- Discuss together why the balloon in the hot water inflates: the hot water heats up the air in the bottle and makes it expand, which blows up the balloon. When you put the bottle into cold water, the air cools down again. Cool air does not have as much energy, so it shrinks and so does the balloon. So, hot air expands and cold air shrinks. (Things that are less dense float on top of things that are more dense, so hot air always floats on cooler air.)

Variations

- Use a marker to write a number on four balloons: 1, 2, 3 and 4. Blow up three balloons and tie them shut. Using a tape measure, find the circumference of each of the three balloons and record their sizes. Place balloon 1 outside of a fridge, balloon 2 inside a freezer, and balloon 3 on the lower shelf of the refrigerator. Shut the doors and wait 30 minutes. Quickly, before the balloons heat up outside the refrigerator, measure the balloons again. Record the measurements. Fit balloon 4 over the mouth of a bottle. Stand the bottle in a bowl and fill the bowl with hot water. Let the bottle stand for one minute. Describe what happens to the balloon. Repeat using iced water.

- Cut shapes (spirals, loops or curves) out of cooking foil and hang them on a piece of thread over a radiator and see what happens. Does the same happen over a cold radiator?

Challenge questions

- Can you find out more about hot air balloons and how they float?
- Can you find out more about birds and hang gliders and how they use hot air?
- Does hot air take up more space than cold air?
- Does the size of the bottle make a difference in this experiment?
- Does the volume of water make a difference?
- If hot air rises, why is it often cold in the mountains?
- Can you find out what 'convection current' means?
- How does underfloor heating work?

Safety consideration

- Be careful when using hot water and make sure children observe from a distance.

Lava lamp

Lava lamp is a fantastic activity for demonstrating the changes that occur when materials are mixed.

Theme

Changing materials

Suitable for

KS1
KS2

Aim

- To describe changes that occur when materials are mixed.

Resources

- Vegetable oil
- Water
- Food colouring (four colours)
- Tall glasses
- Alka-Seltzer tablets
- A real lava lamp

What to do

- Show children a real lava lamp and discuss how it works: the light bulb heats the waxy substance, which causes it to expand and become buoyant so that it floats – after adequate cooling, the waxy substance shrinks and becomes less buoyant again so that it sinks.
- Quarter-fill a tall glass with coloured water.
- Add oil to the glass until it is nearly full – ask children whether oil and water will mix.

- Now add an Alka-Seltzer tablet and see what happens (the tablet will not begin to dissolve until it breaks through and into the water).
- The bubbles of carbon dioxide in the water make buoyant blobs which float in vegetable oil. When the blobs reach the surface, the bubbles pop so the blobs of water become less buoyant and sink again.
- Add different food colours to the lava lamp and see what happens. If the bubbling stops, add some more Alka-Seltzer.
- Explain what is happening and discuss the changes that occur: vegetable oil and water do not mix – the oil floats on water because it is less dense. The chemicals in Alka-Seltzer (it contains bicarbonate of soda) do not dissolve in, and therefore do not react in, vegetable oil. The Alka-Seltzer tablet reacts with the water to make tiny bubbles of carbon dioxide gas. These bubbles attach themselves to the blobs of coloured water and cause them to float to the surface. When the bubbles pop, the coloured blobs sink back to the bottom of the bottle. A real lava lamp works on the same principle of changing the density of something so that it will float and then sink.

Variations

- Use another soluble tablet and see if there is a similar reaction.
- Try using salt instead of a soluble tablet and observe what happens.
- Use different types of oil to test their reaction: for example, baby oil.
- Place a torch under the glass to illuminate the bubbles for maximum effect.

Challenge questions

- Does breaking a soluble tablet into pieces and then placing it into the glass make a difference?
- Is distilled water the best type of water to use?
- Can you write an instruction manual for making a DIY lava lamp?
- Can you make an instructional video for making a DIY lava lamp (for example, for the class on the school's website).
- Who invented the lava lamp?
- Look up the word 'immiscible' – what does it mean?

Put it out

> Put it out is a fizzy science activity for demonstrating how carbon dioxide can be used to extinguish a fire.

Theme

Changing materials

Suitable for

KS1
KS2

Aim

- To understand that non-reversible changes result in the formation of new materials that may be useful.

Resources

- Tealight candle
- Large jam jar
- Water
- Bicarbonate of soda
- Vinegar
- Long match

What to do

- Tell children that the object of the lesson is to extinguish a fire using carbon dioxide.
- Ask children where we would find carbon dioxide and how it can be produced.
- Place a tealight into a jar filled with some water and light the tealight with a long match. Ask children to suggest reasons why the tealight burns? (Air contains oxygen.)
- Next pour some bicarbonate of soda into the water, then add a little vinegar.

- Observe the reaction and ask children to try to explain what has happened.
- Explain the science behind this experiment: when vinegar is combined with bicarbonate of soda, the two react and produce carbon dioxide gas. The carbon dioxide gas is heavier than the surrounding air so it sinks into the bottom of the jar. As the reaction continues, more and more carbon dioxide gas is produced, which begins to slowly fill up the jar. When the level of carbon dioxide has risen to the level of the flame, the flame will go out from lack of air.

Variations

- Repeat the experiment with lemon juice.
- Repeat the experiment with a soluble Alka-Seltzer tablet.
- Repeat the experiment using a large bowl and two candles, one long and one short. Which candle will go out first?
- Have the children take a good look at a fire extinguisher under adult supervision. Why are fire extinguishers always really strong metal canisters? (Because the propellant is stored inside at a high pressure. Strong canisters are needed to stop the extinguishers exploding.)

Challenge questions

- Can you name three different types of fire?
- Can different types of fire be extinguished in the same ways?
- What are carbon dioxide extinguishers commonly used for?
- What is fire?
- What three things does fire need to happen?
- How much carbon dioxide is there in the Earth's atmosphere?
- What colour is carbon dioxide?
- What does carbon dioxide smell of?
- Do animals produce carbon dioxide?
- Can you find out who Antoine Lavoisier is?

Safety considerations

- Only adults are to light the tealights and extinguish them.
- Ensure children understand that a fire extinguisher is a life-saving piece of equipment and not a toy.
- Be careful that children do not inhale the bicarbonate of soda or rub it in their eyes.

Tongue tingle

Tongue tingle is a very easy activity for demonstrating how to make sherbet sizzle in your mouth.

Theme

Changing materials

Suitable for

KS1
KS2

Aim

- To understand that non-reversible changes result in the formation of new materials that may be useful.

Resources

- Icing sugar
- Citric acid
- Bicarbonate of soda
- Spoon
- Large bowl

What to do

- Gather children around you and tell them that you are going to show them how to make sherbet.
- First weigh 100 g of citric acid (citric acid suitable for eating can be easily obtained from a pharmacist).
- Then weigh out 30 g of bicarbonate of soda.
- Next weigh out 200 g of icing sugar. The icing sugar is needed to add sweetness as the citric acid and bicarbonate soda are quite sour. Explain to the children that citric acid is one of the acids found in lemons, oranges and limes; that is why they are called 'citrus fruit'.

- Now mix the ingredients together.
- Ask for volunteer tasters! What do they notice?
- Explain that sherbet fizzes when it comes into contact with moisture on your tongue. It is the carbon dioxide that gives the fizz, forming lots of tiny bubbles directly on your tongue. So where does the fizz come from? It is a reaction between the citric acid and the bicarbonate of soda, which is an alkali.
- Now let children experiment for themselves.

Variations

- The hard part is getting the taste right, so repeat the experiment again by changing the proportions of the three ingredients.
- Try adding flavoured jelly crystals.
- Design some packaging for the sherbet you have created.
- Find the labels from at least ten items of food and drink that contain acids.
- Make a table into which you can put the name of the food or drink and the acid it contains.
- Why do food manufacturers add acids to foods?

Challenge questions

- Can each of the chemicals above make the fizz on their own? Or is a combination of two or all three of them needed? Plan a simple experiment to find out.
- Would heating the mixture make a difference?
- Why is it important to keep the sherbet you have left over in a sealed container?
- Can you find out what a bath bomb is and what happens when one is placed in a bath?

Safety considerations

- Make sure children don't eat too much sherbet at once because it can make your mouth (and stomach) a little sore in very large quantities.
- Be careful that children do not inhale the bicarbonate of soda or rub it in their eyes.

Boil in a bag

> Boil in a bag is a superb multi-sensory activity for demonstrating the water cycle using a plastic bag.

Theme

Changing materials

Suitable for

KS1
KS2

Aim

- To understand the part played by evaporation and condensation in the water cycle.

Resources

- Zipper-style plastic bag
- Medicine cups
- Water
- Food colouring
- Masking tape

What to do

- Tell children that the aim of the lesson is to make a model water cycle.
- Demonstrate first as follows: fill a clear plastic medicine cup half-full with coloured water. This represents the oceans, rivers and lakes.
- Place the cup into a zipper-style plastic bag, taking care not to spill the water. Demonstrate how to hold the bag by one corner so the cup nestles into the bottom corner of the bag. The bag represents the atmosphere and air.
- Blow air inside the bag with your mouth and quickly seal the bag closed.

- Tape the bag directly to a window and periodically look at the bag throughout the day. What changes do you see?
- Some water from the cup should evaporate and condense on the bag (making it appear cloudy), and will then roll down and pool in the bottom of the bag. Look to see if the level of water in the cup is lower. The water on the sides and in the bottom of the bag represents rain. Explain that the water from the cup (representing oceans, rivers, lakes) evaporates into the air in the bag and condenses on the bag (representing clouds). It then runs down inside the bag to the bottom of the bag (representing rain, snow or other precipitation).

Variations

- Repeat the experiment with two bags. Put cold water in the first bag and hot water in the second bag. Compare the two bags.
- Repeat using larger plastic bags. Does that make a difference?
- You could use a bowl of water covered with cling film to show the water cycle.
- A large fish tank can also be used to demonstrate the cycle on a bigger scale.
- Why not draw a simplified picture of the water cycle on the outside of the bag?
- Children could research the Earth's water cycle and design a poster.
- Children could make a cartoon strip of the water cycle from the point of view of a drop of water.
- Children could write and perform a water cycle rap.

Challenge questions

- During what time of the day was evaporation in the bag the greatest?
- During what time of the day was condensation in the bag the greatest?
- Does it matter which window you tape the bag to? Does it have to be, for example, south-facing?
- How does sunlight affect the water cycle?
- Do you think we need to worry about running out of water if the total amount of water on Earth remains constant?
- If water droplets could talk, what would they say to each other?

Safety consideration

- Make sure that the tape you use is strong enough to hold the water cycle bags to the window.

Plastic milk

Plastic milk illustrates how children can make their own plastic using milk and vinegar.

Theme

Changing materials

Suitable for

KS1
KS2

Aim

- To understand what happens to materials when they are mixed.

Resources

- 120 ml of whole milk
- One teaspoon of vinegar
- Small pan
- Small clean jar

What to do

- Tell children that you are going to demonstrate how to make plastic using vinegar and milk.
- Heat the whole milk in a pan until it curdles, or forms lumps.
- Slowly pour off the runny liquid.
- Put the lumps in a jar and add a teaspoon of vinegar. There should be a vinegary reaction that smells.
- Let the mixture stand for an hour or so.
- Slowly pour off any runny liquid inside.
- After an hour or more, a rubbery blob forms in the jar!

- Take the blob out and shape it into a heart, coin, star or some other simple shape. Let it harden in the open jar or on a paper towel for a few hours or longer.
- Once it has dried, you may want to decorate it with acrylic paints.
- Discuss what happens in talking partners and as a class: when the milk and vinegar (or any kind of acid) are mixed together, the milk separates into a liquid and a solid made of fat, minerals, and a protein called casein, which is Latin for cheese. Casein is made up of very long molecules that bend like rubber until they harden. Casein behaves like the plastics that we see in so many objects around us, such as computer keyboards or phones, because it has a similar molecular form.

Variations

- Shape the casein into discs to use as game counters or for decorating.
- Make holes in the middle of the discs to use as buttons. Add colour by rubbing food colouring into the casein before it dries, or by painting the discs once they are dry.

Challenge questions

- Will this experiment work with low-fat milk or soya milk? What about goat's milk or camel's milk?
- Will adding more vinegar make more casein?
- Do all types of vinegar work?
- Will other acids, such as lemon juice and orange juice, work?
- Is casein still used today?
- Who invented plastic?
- What types of plastic are there?
- Can you think of ten uses for plastic?
- What are the benefits of plastic?
- What are the disadvantages of plastic?
- How many tonnes of plastic do we consume in a year?

Safety consideration

- Take care and wear oven gloves when handling anything hot.

Mount Vulcan

Mount Vulcan is a classic science experiment.

Theme

Changing materials

Suitable for

KS1
KS2

Aim

- To understand that changes occur when materials are mixed.

Resources

- Six cups of flour
- Two cups of salt
- Four tablespoons of cooking oil
- Warm water
- Large bowl
- Plastic drinks bottle
- Baking dish or other pan
- Red food colouring
- Washing-up liquid
- Bicarbonate of soda
- Vinegar

What to do

- Discuss with children what volcanoes are, how they are formed, how they erupt and the different types of lava.
- Now show children how to make a model volcano.

- Mix the flour, salt, cooking oil and water by hand in a large bowl until the mixture is smooth and firm to the touch.
- The dough forms the outer surface of the volcano.
- Stand a bottle in a baking pan and mould the dough around it into a volcano shape. Don't cover the hole or drop dough into it.
- Fill the bottle most of the way with warm water and a little red food colouring.
- Add six drops of washing-up liquid to the bottle contents.
- Add two tablespoons of bicarbonate of soda to the liquid.
- Slowly pour vinegar into the bottle and stand back!
- Discuss what science takes place in the experiment: the vinegar and bicarbonate of soda create carbon dioxide and the washing-up liquid causes the volcano to foam up.

Variations

- Play the first part of Igor Stravinsky's *Rite of Spring* and encourage children to pretend they are volcanoes or earthquakes as they move to the music.
- For extra effect you can make a realistic-looking volcano model.
- Take a look at the world's largest vinegar and bicarbonate of soda volcano at www.kptv.com/news/16500941/detail.html.

Challenge questions

- Does vinegar temperature affect how fast the volcano erupts?
- Does the shape of the volcano affect the direction the eruption travels?
- What can be added to the lava to slow it down and make it act more like real lava?
- What combination of vinegar and baking soda creates the biggest eruption?
- What is the world's largest volcano? Where is it?
- What is the largest volcano in our solar system?
- How hot is a volcano?
- Do volcanoes affect the weather?
- Are there any advantages of volcanic eruptions?
- How much of planet Earth is volcanic?
- How can we predict when a volcano will erupt?
- What is the world's most dangerous volcano?

- Which species of bird uses heat given out by warm volcanic sand to incubate its large eggs?
- Why are there no active volcanoes in Australia?
- How fast can lava flow?
- What name do we give to someone who studies volcanoes?
- How many types of volcano are there?
- What percentage of volcanoes are underwater?

Safety considerations

- Care should be taken not to sit too close to the volcano as it may erupt more violently than you think!
- Be careful that children do not inhale the bicarbonate of soda or rub it in their eyes.

Chapter 5
Physical processes
- experiments

'Apparently it is possible to tell what time it is by looking at the sun, but how would you *see* the numbers?'

Raw force

> Raw force is a simple experiment to show the difference between a hard-boiled egg and a raw egg using forces.

Theme

Forces

Suitable for

KS1
KS2

Aim

• To distinguish an uncooked egg from a cooked egg.

Resources

• One raw egg and one hard-boiled egg

What to do

• Spin both eggs and then touch them to stop them moving. Now let go.

• Observe how each egg behaves.

• Encourage children to volunteer their ideas about what they think is happening. Can they spot the difference between the eggs? Which one do they think is cooked?

• Repeat the experiment again.

• Take feedback from children and encourage them to talk together to share ideas.

- Explain what is happening: only the hard-boiled egg spins readily since the mass inside it is solid and evenly distributed. In the case of the raw egg, the fluid inside the raw egg will slide inside the egg as you try to spin it and it causes a drag effect that resists the spin initially. It will eventually spin but the fluid resists coming back to the state of being motionless. So, the egg that spins readily and comes to a stop as soon as it is touched is the hard-boiled egg.

Variations

- Try the experiment again – it is possible to get the hard-boiled egg to stand on its end if it spins at a fast rate.
- Use 12 eggs and ask the children to tell you which one is hard-boiled using what they have learnt.

Challenge questions

- What can you find out about the word 'inertia'? Look up the word in a science dictionary and use the word in an explanation of the experiment above.
- Make a list of other ways you could tell hard-boiled eggs from raw eggs. For example, could you tell by the colour of the egg, the shape, the size?
- How would you tell the difference between a fresh egg and a rotten egg without breaking them? How could you use a bowl of cold water to help you?

Safety considerations

- Make sure that the eggs are cleaned thoroughly before use, or handle them using plastic gloves.
- Dispose of broken eggs safely. Children should not touch raw egg, and should wear plastic gloves to clear away.

A weight off my mind

A weight off my mind is a discussion-based activity to get children talking about the difference between weight and mass.

Theme

Forces

Suitable for

KS1
KS2

Aim

- To draw a distinction between mass and weight.

Resources

- Cards with statements printed on them (see below)

What to do

- Organise the children into groups of two or three.
- Give out the statement cards (copy the statements below and laminate) and ask children to read them together.

    Weight is a force
    Weight is a pull
    Weight is a type of mass
    Weight is not affected by gravity
    An increase in gravity increases an object's mass and weight
    A falling mass has weight because of gravity
    An object has a mass whether or not there is gravity

- Now ask children to discuss which statements they think are correct.

- After a period of discussion in small groups, talk together as a class about each statement in turn and share ideas.
- Give children a further chance to discuss their ideas after listening to the views of others.
- Tell children the difference between mass and weight and share answers.

  Mass is the quantity of matter in an object. The mass of something is always the same. For example, a mass of 1,000 kg on Earth has the same mass on the Moon. However, the weight would be different because the force of gravity is different. The Earth pulls us down and gives us weight. The Moon is smaller than the Earth and has less mass, so an object would weigh about one sixth of its weight on Earth. The force of gravity is the force of attraction between two masses.

  Weight is a force: correct – on Earth it is the pulling force of the Earth's gravity.

  Weight is a pull: correct – weight is a measure of the Earth's pull.

  Weight is a type of mass: incorrect – the weight of an object is a measure of the force of gravity acting on it.

  Weight is not affected by gravity: incorrect – for example, weight is different on Earth and on the Moon.

  An increase in gravity increases an object's mass and weight: incorrect – a greater force of gravity gives an object greater weight, but does not change the amount of matter, the mass, which it has.

  A falling mass has weight because of gravity: any mass has weight, because of the pull of gravity.

  An object has a mass whether or not there is gravity: correct.

Variations

- Limit the number of statements and focus your discussions on just one or two of them.
- Take a vote on each statement and compare results across the class.
- Challenge children to argue and debate for or against their points and try to persuade each other to change their opinions.

Challenge questions

- Can you write a definition of weight and mass for a science dictionary?
- Can you find out what the force of gravity is on other planets in the solar system?
- Can you calculate the weight of a 12 kg mass on Saturn? Mars?
- Can you write some further statements about weight and mass?
- What is the name of the instrument used to measure an object's weight?

Paper tower

Paper tower is a superb hands-on experiment to investigate which shapes make the most stable structures.

Theme

Forces

Suitable for

KS1
KS2

Aims

- To think creatively to try to explain how non-living things work.
- To test ideas using evidence from observation and measurement.
- To use scientific knowledge and understanding to explain observations.

Resources

- Sheets of A4 paper
- Sellotape
- Scissors, rulers, pencils
- Eggs or golf balls

What to do

- Before beginning the investigation, discuss as a class the types of tower seen in the real world and the functions they serve: for example, bell towers (to house bells), watch towers (for observation), lighthouses (for signalling). There are many more types of tower that are used for a wide variety of functions, such as transmission line towers, radar towers, radio and TV broadcasting antenna towers, and towers for suspension bridges. Talk about famous towers such as Blackpool Tower, the Post Office Tower, the Tower of London, the Eiffel Tower, the Tower of Pisa.

- Organise the children into groups of three or four.
- Set the challenge by telling children that it is their mission to build the tallest paper tower they can using five pieces of A4 paper.
- Ask children to make a prediction about how tall a tower they can build. What are their predictions based on?
- Children have a 35-minute period in which to construct their towers.
- Remind children to discuss all the ways they can alter the paper. Encourage them to think about shapes and stability. Reinforce that looking at what other groups are doing is fine and not copying – this is not a competition between groups, but rather a chance to learn from others' discoveries.
- Each tower must be free-standing; it must not be attached to, or lean against, any other surface (floor, wall, desk, etc.). Towers must stand for five seconds. Towers, whether standing straight/erect or sagging/ curved, will be measured from base to highest vertical point. Towers that curve or sag may not be straightened and then measured; they will be measured to the highest vertical point while sagging or curving. The tallest tower wins.

Variations

- Try the experiment above but the tower has to balance an egg or golf ball on top.
- Challenge children to make the tallest paper tower they can using two sheets of newspaper but no tape, staples, glue or other materials.
- Give children £1 per group (plastic money). They can buy extra resources from you, such as paper, paperclips and Sellotape. Invent values for each: for example, paper 50p, paperclips 5p, Sellotape 20p. Groups are penalised by a certain number of centimetres from their tower, according to how much they spend.
- Instead of a tower, groups build trees out of paper with good leaf cover to maximise photosynthesis.

Challenge questions

- How did your result compare to your prediction? Suggest possible reasons for any difference.
- What limited the height of your tower?
- If you could use one other material to make your tower taller, what would it be? Why?
- How well does your tower withstand environmental forces? Use a fan or hairdryer to imitate wind gusts or shake the table gently to imitate an earthquake.
- How can you change your design to better withstand these forces?
- Can you compare how well you can balance with your feet together and then apart? Discuss things that have wide bases for stability (snowshoes, skis, traffic cones). What spacing between your feet feels most stable? How can you apply this knowledge to your paper tower?

Safety considerations

- Make sure that the eggs are cleaned thoroughly before use, or handle them using plastic gloves.
- Dispose of broken eggs safely. Children should not touch raw egg, and should wear plastic gloves to clear away.

Marshmallow tower

> Marshmallow tower is a fantastic hands-on experiment to investigate which shapes make the most stable structures.

Theme

Forces

Suitable for

KS1
KS2

Aims

- To think creatively to try to explain how non-living things work.
- To test ideas using evidence from observation and measurement.
- To use scientific knowledge and understanding to explain observations.

Resources

- Mini-marshmallows
- Cocktail sticks
- Images of famous buildings

What to do

- Organise the children into groups of three or four.
- Set the challenge by telling children that it is their mission to build the tallest free-standing structure from cocktail sticks and marshmallows.
- Demonstrate how to join the sticks and marshmallows together safely.
- Look at some famous structures on the interactive whiteboard sourced through a search engine and talk about the shapes used.
- Encourage children to make sketches of their ideas first before building.

- Distribute materials to children and set a time limit for the completion of the project.
- Measure the heights of each structure and announce the winning team.
- Talk about what worked, what didn't work and how things could be improved.

Variations

- Limit the number of cocktail sticks and mini-marshmallows. Give each stick and marshmallow a value and each group a budget so that they use materials wisely.
- Change the rules so that the structure that can bear the most weight or the one that resembles a famous building is the winner.
- Instead of cocktail sticks, use spaghetti or a combination of the two.

Challenge questions

- How do squares and cubes differ from triangles and pyramids in terms of their overall strength?
- Which is the best pyramid design to use?
- How can extra height be gained?

Safety considerations

- Cocktail sticks are sharp and should be used with great care.
- Children should not eat marshmallows that have been handled many times over.

Water racket

Water racket is an exciting and potentially musical activity that teaches children about sound and pitch using water.

Theme

Light and sound

Suitable for

KS1
KS2

Aims

- To determine whether pitch varies according to the volume of water inside a container.
- To use observations, measurements or other data to draw conclusions.

Resources

- Five empty cans
- Water
- Measuring cylinder/jug
- Plastic ruler
- Wooden ruler

What to do

This experiment could be done as a demonstration or in smaller groups, given enough materials.

- Fill one empty can with water and leave one can empty.
- Pour different amounts of water into the remaining cans.
- Challenge children to predict which can will make the lowest sound and which the highest sound.

- Now tap the side of each can with a ruler. Were they right?
- Play a sound game. Tell the children to stand up if they hear a high sound and to put their hands on their heads if they hear a low sound.
- Now put the cans in order according to the amount of water they contain. Challenge someone to play a tune using the cans.
- Do the children understand that the can with the least amount of water makes the highest note?

Variations

- Instead of using cans, use milk bottles. What difference does the material of the container make? Does blowing across the top of the bottles make the same note as tapping?
- Children could try a similar experiment with different-sized rubber bands and boxes.

Challenge questions

- Does it make a difference whether you use a wooden or plastic ruler?
- Will the sound be different if you use a metal spoon?

Safety considerations

- Ensure that the cans have no sharp edges.
- If you use milk bottles, make sure children do not handle them directly.

On a roll

On a roll is an interesting activity for showing how the contents of a container can change the way it moves. It also encourages children to think carefully about fair testing.

Theme

Forces and motion

Suitable for

KS1
KS2

Aims

- To understand that when objects are pushed or pulled, an opposing pull or push can be felt.
- To understand that friction is a force that slows moving objects.

Resources

- Two cans of tinned tomatoes, soup, baked beans and cat food (they should be the same mass)
- Ramp
- Books
- Rulers/metre sticks

What to do

- Remove the labels from the cans and mark them in some way so that you know what their contents are (for example, with a letter marked on the base).
- Tell children that they are going to investigate how far some food cans will go after being rolled down a slope. Say that you don't know what is inside the cans but that they all have the same mass.

- Set up the ramp, using books to rest the ramp on.
- Before rolling the first can, ask children to think of the variables involved. What is the one thing that will be changed each time? How will they measure? What variables do they need to control in order to make the test fair?
- Now roll the cans and see how far they travel.
- Discuss why some may roll further than others.

Variations

- Ramps made of different materials could be used.
- Different-sized cans could be used and compared.
- Instead of rolling, let the cans slide down the ramp on their ends.

Challenge questions

- Why don't the cans roll the same distance, despite being launched from the same height?
- Can you guess what might be inside the unlabelled cans?

Safety considerations

- Ensure that the ramp is set up away from anything fragile.
- Make sure the cans don't pick up enough speed to hurt anyone.

Check canopy

Check canopy allows children to work systematically within the context of a structured investigation to test parachute descent.

Theme

Forces and motion

Suitable for

KS1
KS2

Aims

- To understand that objects are pulled downwards because of the gravitational attraction between them and Earth.
- To understand air resistance as a force that slows moving objects and may prevent objects from starting to move.

Resources

- Different materials to form parachute canopies, such as tissue paper, cellophane, bin liners, tissue paper, aluminium foil
- Cotton thread, string, wool
- Scissors
- Blu-tack

What to do

- Tell children that they are going to make some parachutes and test which material is the best for the canopy.
- Organise the children into groups of three and distribute the materials.

- Take ideas from groups about which variables need to be kept the same in their experiments and which variable is the one that will be systematically changed each time.
- Let children cut their canopies into square shapes of their own dimensions.
- Demonstrate how to tie a thread into each corner and how to attach to the Blu-tack.
- Let children test their parachutes from a safe height: for example, standing on a chair and launching.
- Compare the performance of the parachutes and discuss what problems were encountered in the investigation.

Variations

- Try changing the size of the canopies to see whether that makes a difference.
- Try changing the thread. Does it matter if wool is used? String? And so on.
- Try changing the mass of the Blu-tack and the height from which the parachute is launched.

Challenge questions

- How do you think the descent of the parachute will be affected by cutting a small hole in the centre of the canopy?
- How do you think using only three pieces of thread will alter the descent of the parachute?
- Does it make a difference if the same person is testing the parachute each time?

Safety considerations

- Warn children about climbing onto their chairs safely.
- Be careful that children do not to throw the parachute towards anyone.
- Be vigilant when children are using scissors to cut the canopies.

Bubble trouble

Bubble trouble is a great soap science activity for finding out how bubbles move under different conditions.

Theme

Forces and motion

Suitable for

KS1
KS2

Aim

- To explore and investigate how bubbles move in different conditions.

Resources

- Bubble mixture (washing-up liquid and water)
- Hoops to blow the bubble mixture through
- Sheets of card

What to do

- Give out the bubble mixture and hoops and let children practise blowing bubbles. Demonstrate how to do this if children are unsure what to do.

- After a while, tell children to blow a stream of bubbles and ask everyone to observe how they move.

- Now challenge children to speed up the way the bubbles move. Can they make the bubbles change direction and travel upwards?

- Ask children whether the size of bubbles makes a difference to the way they move and fall.

Variations

- Try using different bubble mixtures (dilute and concentrate) and making your own bubble solution recipes.
- Compare and contrast some of the top brands of commercial washing-up liquid and the bubbles they make.
- Try using different-sized bubble hoops and hoops made from different materials.

Challenge questions

- Would it make a difference if the experiment was done in different rooms?
- Would it make a difference if the experiment was done outside?
- What could you do to make the bubbles change direction? For example, use sheets of card as flappers.
- What is inside a bubble?
- Are all bubbles made of soap?
- What types of bubbles can you think of that you have seen before? For example, fizzy drink bubbles.
- How are bubbles and balloons alike and how are they different?
- Can you compose a poem about bubbles?

Safety consideration

- Remind children to blow the bubble mixture away from other people's eyes.

Rocket balloon

Rocket balloon demonstrates the pushing force of thrust and teaches children about the importance of fair testing.

Theme

Forces

Suitable for

KS1
KS2

Aim

- To explore types of force and to understand that, when objects are pushed or pulled, an opposing pull or push can be felt.

Resources

- Balloons (round ones will work, but the longer airship or sausage balloons work best)
- Long pieces of kite string or fishing wire (about 10–15 feet long)
- Plastic straws
- Tape
- Tape measures
- Stopwatches

What to do

- Tie one end of a piece of string to a chair, door knob or other support.
- Put the other end of the string through a straw.
- Pull the string tight and tie it to another support in the room.
- Blow up a balloon (but don't tie it). Pinch the end of the balloon (or put a peg over the end) and tape the balloon to the straw.
- Countdown from five and then let go!

- Discuss the demonstration and explain the science at work: when the air from the balloon rushes out backwards, it propels the 'rocket' forwards. If the friction between the wire and the straw is high then the rocket will go just a short distance. However, if the friction is low then the rocket will go much further. Gases tend to move from areas of high pressure to areas of low pressure. The air inside the balloon is compressed and under more pressure than the air outside, so it tries to escape when you release the balloon. As the gas is released from the balloon, it creates thrust. This can be explained by Newton's Third Law of Motion: for every action there is an equal and opposite reaction.
- Now let children have a go themselves and have a competition using tape measures and stopwatches to see who can create the fastest rocket.

Variations

- Try rubbing a little washing-up liquid on the wire first and see what happens when you launch your balloon.
- This experiment can be extended by measuring the distance the balloon travels in metres and dividing it by the time taken in seconds. This gives the average velocity of the balloon over the course of the journey in metres per second.

Challenge questions

- Does the shape of the balloon affect how far (or fast) the rocket travels?
- Does the length of the straw affect how far (or fast) the rocket travels?
- Does the type of string affect how far (or fast) the rocket travels? Try fishing line, nylon string, cotton string, etc.
- Does the angle of the string affect how far (or fast) the rocket travels?
- If you keep using the same balloon, will its increased stretchiness alter its performance?
- Can you design a paper rocket to stick to your balloon?

Safety considerations

- Tie the wire to something that will not open, such as a door into the classroom.
- Everyone should work with enough space around them.

What do you flink?

What do you flink? is a forces-based challenge in which children try to make an object suspend itself in water, neither floating nor sinking but 'flinking'!

Theme

Forces

Suitable for

KS1
KS2

Aim

- To explore types of force and to understand that, when objects are pushed or pulled, an opposing pull or push can be felt.

Resources

- Styrofoam packing peanuts
- Paperclips
- Clear containers
- Water

What to do

- Demonstrate to children that when you drop a foam peanut into a container of water it floats and that when you drop a paperclip into the same container it sinks.

- Challenge children to think of a way of making the foam 'flink', i.e. suspend itself in the middle of the container without floating or sinking. They could discuss their ideas with a partner.

- Distribute the activity materials to the pairs and cover tables with newspaper to soak up any water spills.

- The secret of making this work is to adjust the amount of foam peanuts and paperclips. Children will have to bend the paperclips and manipulate them to make the peanuts flink.
- Once a child makes a flinker, ask them to share with the rest of the class how to do it.

Variations

- Encourage children to repeat the activity with other materials such as sponges, wine corks or plastic bottle caps.
- Instead of water, they could use some different solutions and compare any differences.
- Can they make a helium balloon flink?

Challenge questions

- Does it matter what type of water is used? For example, does carbonated water give different results than still water?
- Can you think of something in real life that behaves like a 'flinker' (for example, a submarine)?
- Can you find out what ballast tanks are used for?

Magic paperclips

Magic paperclips is an excellent activity to demonstrate surface tension using paperclips and water.

Theme

Forces

Suitable for

KS1
KS2

Aim

- To explore types of force and to understand that, when objects are pushed or pulled, an opposing pull or push can be felt.

Resources

- Clean, dry paperclips
- Tissue paper
- Bowls of water

What to do

- Fill a bowl with water and ask a volunteer to try and make the paperclip float. Discuss as a class why the paperclip sinks and ask for ideas about how to make the paperclip float.
- Now tear a piece of tissue paper and gently place it on top of the surface of the water.
- Next very carefully place a dry paperclip flat onto the tissue, trying not to touch the water or the tissue.
- Now poke the tissue with a pencil to make the paper sink. With care, the tissue will sink and leave the paperclip floating.

- Now set children off to do the same and see if they can make the paperclip float.
- After children have had a go themselves, discuss the science at work. How can the paperclip float? Explain that there is a sort of skin on the surface of water where the water molecules hold tightly together. If the conditions are right, they can hold tightly enough to support a paperclip. The paperclip is not truly floating, it is being held up by this surface tension.

Variations

- Try opening the paperclip to see if it can float.
- Try rubbing the paperclip with a candle.
- Try to float other lightweight household items on the water and see what happens.
- Try putting the paperclip into another liquid, such as vegetable oil.

Challenge questions

- How many paperclips can the surface tension hold?
- Does the shape of the paperclip affect its floating ability?
- Does the water have to be especially clean?
- Which liquids have the strongest surface tension?
- How can the surface tension of water be made stronger? For example, try sprinkling baby powder on the surface and see what happens.
- Can you think of any insects that might use surface tension to walk across water? How do they do it without tissue paper?
- Could this be done with an object larger than a paperclip? If so, what would it be?

Flying paperclip

Flying paperclip is a fabulous scientific trick that uses magnetism to wow children.

Theme

Forces

Suitable for

KS1
KS2

Aim

- To explore types of force and that when objects are pushed or pulled, an opposing pull or push can be felt.

Resources

- Clean, dry paperclips
- Scissors
- Thread
- Sellotape
- Clean, empty glass jars with metal lids
- Magnets

What to do

- Cut a piece of thread a few centimetres long and tie one end to a paperclip. Tape the other end to the bottom of a jar.
- Place a magnet inside the lid and show everyone the jar with the clip lying at the bottom of the jar.
- Screw the lid on the jar, and then turn the jar upside down so the clip hangs from the string.

- Turn the jar right side up again and the paperclip remains suspended in air.
- Discuss why this works: the magnet attracts the paperclip, but the thread prevents the paperclip from being pulled to the magnet.
- Children can now try this for themselves with a partner.
- Ask children to write and illustrate what they did in this experiment and what they learned. Emphasise that written explanations should include a description of a magnetic field and a summary of what they learned about each of the materials used to test the magnetic field.

Variations

- Repeat this experiment by inserting a piece of paper between the paperclip and the magnet. Test your prediction. Try using a range of other materials and observe what happens.
- Try using different paperclips and a different container.

Challenge questions

- Can you list ten other objects that you can substitute for the paperclip?
- What would happen if you took a pair of scissors and then cut through the gap between the paperclip and the magnet?
- Does the type of magnet make a difference to this experiment?

Safety consideration

- Magnets will disrupt or damage computer monitors and magnetic storage media.

Cola float

Cola float is a very simple but engaging experiment to demonstrate the density of different liquids.

Theme

Forces

Suitable for

KS1
KS2

Aim

- To measure forces and identify the direction in which they act.

Resources

- Can of regular cola
- Can of diet cola
- Fish tank
- Water

What to do

- Show children two cans of cola, one diet and one regular. The cans should have exactly the same volume or size. Ask children to predict whether the cans will float or sink.

- Then place the regular cola into a tank of deep water and observe what happens – it sinks. Ask the children to say what they think will happen to the diet cola.

- Place the diet cola into the water and watch what happens – it floats.

- Challenge children to think why this happens.

- Share ideas around the class.
- Now explain the reason why one sinks and the other floats: the high sugar content in regular cola makes it more dense. Diet colas are less dense because the artificial sweetener used is much sweeter than sugar, and so it is not necessary to add nearly as much (about ten times less). So diet colas are less dense than regular cola, and a can of diet cola will float in water but not a can of regular cola.

Variations

- Repeat this experiment with other drinks, such as lemonade or fizzy orange.
- Use the product nutrition labels to record the liquid volume in millilitres (ml) and the mass of each cola (sugar) in grams (g).

Challenge questions

- What makes the regular cola sink, apart from the sugar content?
- Do all fizzy drinks that contain sugar sink?
- Are there any varieties of regular pop that will float?
- Are there any varieties of diet drink that sink?
- Can you think of other factors that might influence which sodas float or sink?
- Does the shape of the can make a difference to whether it floats or sinks?
- How could you make a can of regular cola float without opening the can? For example, how would bubble wrap help?

Floating in air

Floating in air is a fun activity for exploring air pressure.

Theme

Forces and motion

Suitable for

KS1
KS2

Aims

- To understand that when objects are pushed or pulled, an opposing pull or push can be felt.
- To measure forces and identify the direction in which they act.

Resources

- Ping pong balls
- Hairdryer
- Paper towel tubes

What to do

- Tell children that you are going to demonstrate how a ping pong ball can defy gravity.
- Turn the hairdryer on high and point it toward the ceiling. Make sure to use a cool-air setting.
- Ask children what they think will happen if you gently place the ping pong ball into the stream of air. Will it blow away, drop to the floor or float? Now try it and see.
- Try walking slowly, tilting or jiggling the hair dryer. What happens to the ball?

- Discuss as a class what is happening in the experiment: when you place the ball in the stream of air created by the hairdryer, you force the air to flow around the ball and create an area of lower pressure. The still air surrounding the air stream has more pressure and pushes the ball to keep it snuggled in the stream.
- Now try slowly lowering an empty paper towel tube over the ball. What happens now? (The air is funnelled into a smaller area, making air move even faster. The pressure in the tube becomes even lower than that of the air surrounding the ball, and the ball is sucked up into the tube.)

Variations

- Try to float two or more balls in the same air stream. How many can you float at once? How do they behave when there is more than one?
- Try tubes that are longer or shorter or wider or skinnier.
- Try to float other objects in the air stream, such as a small balloon.

Challenge questions

- In what ways did this activity help you better understand the force of gravity?
- Can you find out about a Swiss scientist called Bernoulli?
- Can you find out how this experiment would help aeronautic engineers design aeroplane wings?

Safety considerations

- Use a hairdryer that is approved as safe for use in schools.
- Do not use the hairdryer near water.

Uphill struggle

Uphill struggle makes children do a double-take by demonstrating how things can roll uphill.

Theme

Forces and motion

Suitable for

KS1
KS2

Aims

- To understand that when objects are pushed or pulled, an opposing pull or push can be felt.
- To measure forces and identify the direction in which they act.

Resources

- Two metre-long rulers or long pieces of wood joined together
- Two identical funnels taped together
- Blocks or books to raise the end of the rulers
- Rubber band

What to do

- Tell children that you are going to make an gravity-defying device out of two large funnels taped together.
- Take two metre sticks, and place them on a table to form an open-ended triangle, with the open end of the triangle raised up on one or two books. Hold the bottom ends of the rulers together with a rubber band.

- Place two funnels taped together at the bottom part of the triangle track. Slowly pull the rulers apart and watch it roll uphill!
- Explain that the funnels do not really roll uphill. It is actually a visual illusion because as the gap widens the funnels drop slightly and spin forwards.

Variations

- To appreciate this experiment further, discuss what gravity hills are: at several hilly locations around the USA, objects such as cars left in neutral gear supposedly roll uphill. However, GPS measurements confirm that the effects are illusions caused by the landscape: the position of trees and slopes of nearby scenery, or a curvy horizon line, can blend to trick the eye so that what looks uphill is actually downhill.
- Look at the link about the Electric Brae in Scotland www. undiscoveredscotland.co.uk/dunure/electricbrae/index.html
- Watch a video clip of a car appearing to move uphill by following the link www.aip.org/dbis/stories/2006/15183.html

Challenge questions

- Does the length of the rulers make a difference to the experiment?
- Does the height of the books influence the movement of the funnel?
- Do the types of funnel make a difference?
- What else could you use instead of funnels?

Sticky situation

Sticky situation is a simple but clever experiment to demonstrate surface tension.

Theme

Forces and motion

Suitable for

KS1
KS2

Aim

- To recognise differences between solids, liquids and gases, in terms of ease of flow and maintenance of shape and volume.

Resources

- Drinks carton or milk carton
- Water
- Measuring jug
- Masking tape

What to do

- Before the experiment, wash a drinks carton thoroughly and then make four small holes in a row at the bottom of the carton about 1 cm apart.
- Now tape over the holes using masking tape.
- Fill a measuring jug with water then pour the water into the carton.
- Remove the tape and watch the water come out in streams.
- Repeat the experiment: dry the carton, place fresh masking tape over the holes and fill the carton with water.

- Challenge the children to think of a way to make the four streams join together to make one stream.
- This time when you remove the masking tape, pinch the streams together and see what happens.
- Explain that surface tension is a special attribute of water. When water is exposed to air, it forms a thin 'skin' that keeps the water together. This is how some insects skim over a water's surface: surface tension keeps them from sinking into the water. The streams of water are held together, once they have been joined, by the water's stickiness, or surface tension.

Variations

- Repeat the experiment with three holes 2 cm apart – when you pinch the water, do the streams join together?
- Repeat the experiment with two holes 3 cm apart.

Challenge questions

- Do the streams stay joined together even if you move your fingers away?
- How close do the holes have to be for the experiment to work?
- Would this work for another solution? For example, what would happen if you tried milk?
- Would you say that water is sticky? Explain this concept to a science partner.

In a spin

In a spin is an illustration of the principle 'every action has an equal and opposite reaction'.

Theme

Forces and motion

Suitable for

KS1
KS2

Aims

- To understand that when objects are pushed or pulled, an opposing pull or push can be felt.
- To understand how to measure forces and identify the direction in which they act.

Resources

- Empty one-litre fruit juice carton
- Piece of string
- Pair of scissors
- Washing-up bowl
- Water

What to do

- Make a hole in the bottom left-hand corner of each of the four faces of a one-litre juice carton. Poke two holes either side at the top of the carton and tie a piece of string through it.
- Knot the string, so that you can hang the carton from it.
- Next pour some water into the washing-up bowl so that it's about a quarter-full.

- Now place the carton into the bowl of water.
- Then pour water into the carton until it is full.
- If you lift the carton out of the water by the string, the carton should spin around.
- Discuss together why the carton spins around: water shoots out the holes, and pushes back on the carton with equal force. A sort of turbine is made as the energy of the moving liquid is turned into rotational energy.

Variations

- Try doing the experiment with fewer holes or more holes and see what happens.
- Try the experiment again with larger holes.
- Repeat the experiment by putting the holes in the bottom right-hand corners of the carton.
- Place the holes in the middle of the carton.

Challenge questions

- Can you see why you put water in the bowl before placing the carton in the bowl of water? (So that you can fill up the carton without water pouring straight out of the holes.)
- Can you find out who Hero of Alexandria was and what he discovered?
- Does the length of string make a difference to how the carton turns?
- If you did this experiment in the southern hemisphere, would you expect the carton to spin in the opposite direction?

Mobile disco

Mobile disco is a brilliant experiment for demonstrating vibration and sound.

Theme

Light and sound

Suitable for

KS1
KS2

Aims

- To understand that sounds are made when objects vibrate but that vibrations are not always directly visible.
- To understand that vibrations from sound sources require a medium through which to travel to the ear.

Resources

- Two mobile phones
- Large drinking glass
- Cling film
- Salt and pepper

What to do

- Explain to children that the object of the lesson is to build a salt and pepper disco.
- Select a suitable ringtone and place your mobile phone inside a dry, empty drinking glass.
- Now make your dance floor by stretching cling film taut across the mouth of the glass like a drum.

- Sprinkle some salt and pepper on the cling wrap.
- Now use a second phone to ring the mobile phone inside the glass.
- When it starts ringing, the salt and pepper start to boogie!
- Explain the science involved and talk together about what is happening: sound is based on vibration. When any object vibrates, it causes movement in the air particles. These particles bump into other particles nearby and they vibrate, too. The plastic cling film vibrates, and makes the pepper dance. This movement keeps going until the particles run out of energy.

Variations

- Make some tiny paper dancers to stand on the dance floor.
- Try other materials and test whether they can dance too, such as dust, glitter, rice crispies and so on.
- Ask children to draw and label a picture that shows what makes the salt and pepper dance. They should explain their drawings to the rest of the class.
- Look at words that imitate the sounds they represent, such as hiss, rustle, growl and chirp. Encourage children to find other onomatopoeic words to enrich their writing.

Challenge questions

- Does the volume setting on the phone make a difference to this experiment?
- Does the container make a difference? What would happen if you used a different material to put the mobile phone into?
- Does the tautness of the cling film make a difference?
- What else could you use for a dance floor instead of cling film?
- What is sound? Can you write a definition for a science dictionary?
- How many different ways do you use vibration in your daily life?

What's the time?

What's the time? is a brilliant experiment to show how a potato can be turned into a battery to operate a clock.

Theme

Electricity

Suitable for

KS1
KS2

Aim

- To construct circuits, incorporating a battery or power supply and a range of switches, to make electrical devices work.

Resources

- Potatoes
- Plates
- Pennies
- Galvanised nails
- Three lengths of insulated copper wire, each with two inches of the insulation stripped off one end
- Digital clock with attachments for wires

What to do

- Cut a potato in half and put the two halves on a plate so they stand on their flat ends.
- Next wrap the end of one piece of wire around a galvanised nail and wrap the end of a second piece of wire around a penny.
- Then stick the nail and penny into one half of the potato so that they are not touching each other.

- Next wrap a third piece of wire around another penny and put it into the other half of the potato. Put another nail into the second half of the potato, but this nail should not have wire wrapped around it.
- Now connect the wire from the penny on the first half of the potato to the nail that has no wire on it in the second half of the potato.
- Finally, touch the free ends of the wires to the wires coming out of the digital clock.
- Discuss how the potato battery works: a potato battery is an 'electrochemical' battery. An electrochemical cell is a battery in which chemical energy is converted to electric energy.

Variations

- Try using different types of potato and see if they work in the same way.
- Try using other things that could act as a battery: for example, pears, lemons, bananas. Do they all work?
- Some metals make better batteries than others. Try to find a combination of metals that gives the most voltage and current.

Challenge questions

- Does the size of a potato make a difference?
- Does the type of potato make a difference?
- Does the age of a potato make a difference?
- Why would it be a good idea to scuff the nail and copper wire with sandpaper or steel wool until it is shiny?
- How could you measure the amount of electricity produced?
- Can you make a circuit using potatoes to make a light and buzzer work?
- How does a battery work?
- What is current?
- What is voltage?
- What happens when you put two batteries in series?
- What happens when you put two batteries in parallel?
- Who invented the battery?

Safety consideration

- Dispose of the potatoes after the experiment; do not eat them.

Chapter 6
Games

'When people run around and around in circles we say they are crazy. When planets do it we say they are orbiting.'

Introduction

In this chapter you will find a collection of tried and tested literacy-linked science games. The games provide an enjoyable way for children to consolidate and build their word power, vocabulary and creative thinking while having fun. The games all share the same aims and have been designed to be as practical as possible.

You can use a game as part of your lesson or for a session at the end of the day. Many of the games help lay a foundation for further science work by allowing children to see connections between concepts. Children will be talking and sharing with others, using the medium of science and scientific language. When used regularly, these games will help to improve children's knowledge, understanding and confidence.

Top trumps

Top trumps is a scientific adaptation of the well-known card game. The cards are great ways of improving children's knowledge and understanding, and it helps them to read and compare numbers more confidently.

Suitable for

KS1
KS2

Aims

- To enrich vocabularies and improve understanding of scientific terms.
- To articulate, qualify and justify thinking.
- To strengthen connections between key concepts and ideas.
- To consider what sources of information they will use to answer questions.

Organisation

- This is suitable for small groups of two to four

Resources

- Top trumps cards

What to do

- Show children some actual Top Trump cards – you could ask children to bring in their own and explain to the class how they are played, i.e. each card contains a list of numerical data, and the aim of the game is to compare these values in order to try to trump and win an opponent's card.
- Using the same formula as the classic card game of Top Trumps, create some cards according to the topic you are studying or revising.

- Here are some Top Trump examples for mini-beasts. These can be used as starting points for discussion and further research for children to create their own.

Stick Insect

Body segments:	3
Legs:	6
Wings:	4
Length:	30–320 mm
Width:	3 mm
Habitat:	branches, leaves, grass
Diet:	herbivore
Harmful:	cannot bite or sting

Grasshopper

Body segments:	3
Legs:	6
Wings:	4
Length:	20 mm
Width:	5 mm
Habitat:	fields, meadows, mountains, forests, deserts
Diet:	herbivore
Harmful:	can bite

Dragonfly

Body segments:	3
Legs:	6
Wings:	4
Length:	80 mm
Width:	50 mm
Habitat:	ponds, lakes, canals, rivers, ditches, bogs
Diet:	carnivore
Harmful:	does not bite or sting

- Children can then play a game of top trumps and discuss whether or not they agree with the ratings for each category.

Variations

- Top trumps cards can be made for any topic. For example, the topic could be nutrition and staying healthy. Create one card per food or meal and include a number of categories: for example, calories, sugar, salt. Then allocate a point score for each of the categories ranging from 1 (not good) up to 20 (really good).
- The cards can be laminated so they can be used again and again.

Who wants to be a science millionaire?

Who wants to be a science millionaire? is a classic multiple-choice game that can help children learn new concepts and improve their understanding.

Suitable for

KS1
KS2

Aims

- To enrich vocabularies and improve understanding of scientific terms.
- To articulate, qualify and justify thinking.
- To strengthen connections between key concepts and ideas.
- To consider what sources of information they will use to answer questions .

Organisation

- This is suitable for small groups of two to four

Resources

- Who wants to be a science millionaire? template

What to do

- Show children an example of a 'Who wants to be a millionaire?' game made up of science questions. There are lots of PowerPoint millionaire games to be found on the internet. (Try this one from Mark E. Damon on plants http://teach.fcps.net/trt2/activities/Plant%20Millionaire.ppt)
- Now challenge children to think of their own versions for the topic you are studying.
- You can provide a list of questions to get children going.

- Explain to children that the idea of the game is to have one correct answer and three distractors. Talk about what makes a good question and what make good multiple-choice answers. Explain that questions and answers work well when a little humour is embedded in them as it makes things more memorable.

1. What causes night and day?
    a) God turns the lights on and off.
    b) The Earth moves around the Sun.
    c) The Earth spins on its axis.
    d) The Sun goes round the Earth.

    _ Other answers you could include here are: 'Clouds block out the Sun's light', 'The Earth moves into and out of the Sun's shadow', 'The Sun goes to sleep', 'The Moon gets in the way', and so on.

2. Which of these statements is correct about the Earth's Moon?
    a) It is a planet.
    b) It is a star.
    c) It is a satellite.
    d) It is a lump of green cheese.

3. Why does a solar eclipse happen?
    a) The Sun goes behind Mercury.
    b) The Moon comes between the Sun and the Earth.
    c) The Sun shrinks for 24 hours.
    d) The Earth faces away from the Sun.

Variations

- Invent your own rules. For example, traditionally such games have four multiple-choice options but you could have three or five. You could have a 75:25 option where one answer is removed instead of two in 50:50. Instead of phone a friend, you could 'phone an expert'. If you can't answer a question then you can say 'Pass' but you lose two lifelines. You could also have fewer questions or more questions.

Squares

Squares is a game in which contestants must answer trivia questions to complete a path across or down a game board of squares. This activity works well for using in science and is especially suited to revision.

Suitable for

KS1
KS2

Aims

- To enrich vocabularies and improve understanding of scientific terms.
- To articulate, qualify and justify thinking.
- To strengthen connections between key concepts and ideas.
- To consider what sources of information they will use to answer questions.

Organisation

- This is suitable for small groups of two to four

Resources

- Squares template

What to do

- Explain how the game works: teams compete against each other to move across or down the board, linking squares together in a continuous chain.
- Split the class into two teams.
- Each team needs a spokesperson.

- The first team picks a letter from the squares grid. The grid can be created and photocopied or played onscreen. Making the squares grids can be time consuming; for free grids on a range of science topics go to www.teachers-direct.co.uk/resources/quiz-busters/quiz-busters-directory.aspx

- Read out the accompanying question to that letter (you will need to create these). Read your questions in the same style: 'Which C is the word to describe a gas turning into a liquid?', 'Which D describes ...?', 'Which F stands for ...?'

- The team confer and the spokesperson gives the answer. If they get it wrong, the other team have a go.

- If both teams get it wrong, ask another question beginning with the same letter, until that letter is 'won'.

- Continue until one team has a line either vertically or horizontally.

- Play can be the best of three games.

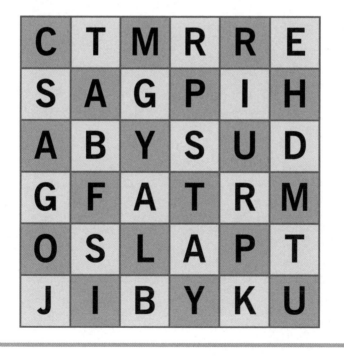

Variations

- If you print off any boards you make or download, then laminate them so they can be re-used.
- Adapt the rules: have a hotspot letter which, if answered correctly, means the next square can be covered.
- Alter the grid size.

Family fortunes

Family fortunes is another classic adaptation of a popular game show where two teams are asked to guess the results of surveys in which 100 people are asked a question.

Suitable for

KS1
KS2

Aims

- To enrich vocabularies and improve understanding of scientific terms.
- To articulate, qualify and justify thinking.
- To strengthen connections between key concepts and ideas.
- To consider what sources of information they will use to answer questions.

Organisation

- This is suitable for small groups of two to four

Resources

- No special resources needed

What to do

- Ask children to get into teams of five or six and give themselves a team name.
- Explain how the game works: teams are asked questions from a fictitious survey of 100 people. For example, 'According to 100 scientists surveyed, can you name five cold-blooded animals?'
- Children have a few minutes to confer with each other and then a spokesperson gives an answer on behalf of their team.

- If the answer is correct then that team gains control of the board. (The numbers after each answer relate to the number of scientists who out of 100 answered with that particular response. These equate to points.)

- The team with control of the board is asked to think of the remaining answers, and if they guess correctly, then they win the game.

- If a team doesn't guess correctly, play passes over to the other team, which has the chance to answer and win the game.

- You will need to think carefully about what answers to include. This gives you the opportunity to include the most common answers but also some less well-known answers that might surprise children. So, to answer the question above, five possible answers might be:

1. Fish (69)
2. Snakes (15)
3. Frogs (9)
4. Dragonflies (5)
5. Bees (2)

Variations

- Bonus points can be given for definitions of words. So, for the example below, teams can earn 20 extra points if they can define the parts of the flower they name.

  'According to 100 scientists surveyed, what are the top four parts of a flower?'

  1. Petals (72)
  2. Stamen (12)
  3. Carpel (11)
  4. Sepal (5)

- Challenge children to invent their own questions and points system.

Show me

Show me is a knock-out game in which children answer a variety of questions until there is just one outright winner left.

Suitable for

KS1
KS2

Aims

- To enrich vocabularies and improve understanding of scientific terms.
- To articulate, qualify and justify thinking.
- To strengthen connections between key concepts and ideas.
- To consider what sources of information they will use to answer questions.

Organisation

- This is suitable as a whole-class activity

Resources

- Mini-whiteboard marker pens and erasers

What to do

- Prepare a list of graded questions based upon the content of previous lessons. Make your questions short and direct or devise questions with a choice of two answers. For example:

    Is a dolphin a fish or a mammal?
    What does a carnivore eat, plants or animals?
    How many bones are there in the adult human skeleton?

- Give each pupil a mini-whiteboard/marker pen/eraser.

- Children all stand up and write their answers to the questions you ask on their boards and then hold them up at the same time when you say 'Show me'. Children with an incorrect answer have to sit down.
- Play continues until there is just one person standing.

Variations

- Children can work in pairs rather than individually and so share ideas.
- Questions can be given with multiple-choice answers so that responses are written as A, B, C or D.
- If you have a mixed class you could play the game as boys versus girls.

Are you smarter than a Year 6 pupil?

This game is inspired by the American TV show *Are You Smarter than a Fifth Grader?*

Suitable for

KS2

Aims

- To enrich vocabularies and improve understanding of scientific terms.
- To articulate, qualify and justify thinking.
- To strengthen connections between key concepts and ideas.
- To consider what sources of information they will use to answer questions.

Organisation

- This is suitable as a whole-class activity

Resources

- PowerPoint presentation of questions

What to do

- The game can be played using a PowerPoint presentation. Tell children that you have a number of questions that have been answered by someone in Year 6 (or choose Year 7 if you are in Year 6) and you would like them to answer the same questions. The aim is to try and do better than the Year 6 pupil who has already answered.

- You can show them a presentation of a series of questions related to the topic you are studying or revising. Questions can be a mixture of words, pictures and graphs. For example, find four pictures of different shaped fish and ask the question: 'Some fish are streamlined so they can move quickly in water. Which of these fish probably moves the quickest?' Children then answer working in teams and compete against each other.

- Tell children that they have to get ten continuous correct answers to beat the Year 6 pupil.

Variations

- You could include questions on spellings, definitions or science in the news.
- Use video clips or images from websites as a stimulus for a question.
- You could play this game as Beat the Teacher where teams research questions they could ask you about the topic being studied. Children write questions and answers and nominate one person to challenge you. This stretches children as they try to devise difficult questions to outwit you.

Call my science bluff

Call my science bluff involves teams taking it in turns to provide three definitions of a science word, only one of which is correct. The other team then has to guess which is the correct definition.

Suitable for

KS2

Aims

- To enrich vocabularies and improve understanding of scientific terms.
- To articulate, qualify and justify thinking.
- To strengthen connections between key concepts and ideas.
- To consider what sources of information they will use to answer questions.

Organisation

- This is suitable for the whole class or small teams

Resources

- Whiteboard and pens
- Science word mats and dictionaries

What to do

- Children are split into teams of four. Each team should select a science word from a word mat or science dictionary.
- Three members of the team should write on a whiteboard a false definition for the word and an example of usage (they could include pronunciation and information about what part of speech the word is).
- The aim is to make the definitions as credible as possible. The fourth member of the team rewrites the correct dictionary definition in the same style as the other definitions.

- Each team member then reads out their definition and after a period of consultation, a class vote is taken on which one sounds the most credible. These can be formal or informal in nature or a mixture of both. For example:

What is an ammeter?

1. A device for measuring the force of gravity.
2. An instrument for measuring electrical currents.
3. A type of thermometer used for measuring outside temperatures.
4. A meter that measures time but only in the morning.

What is the meaning of sonorous?

1. A sonorous is a cross between a rhinoceros and a hippopotamus.
2. Sonorous refers to the pinging sound when a metal has been hit.
3. The sonorous is the name given to the space between your eyebrows.
4. Sonorous is the name of a scientific rock group.

What does 'surface tension' mean?

1. The movement of the facial muscles when under stress.
2. A tendency for a plant's roots to grow to the top of a plant pot.
3. The way molecules are attracted to each other on the top of a liquid to make a skin.
4. It's like standing to attention, but lying down.

Variations

- There are many ways to pose a question for this game: for example, 'Which of these is the definition for opaque?', 'What does an optician do?', 'What is the definition of the word conductor?', 'What does the word precipitation refer to?'
- You could include four definitions instead of three.
- Teams can create a collection of examples and then play against each other.
- Examples can be created for a display or competition or for a science/school newsletter/website.

You say, we pay!

Based on the TV game, this game involves children describing an object or idea without using the word itself.

Suitable for

KS1
KS2

Aims

- To enrich vocabularies and improve understanding of scientific terms.
- To articulate, qualify and justify thinking.
- To strengthen connections between key concepts and ideas.
- To consider what sources of information they will use to answer questions.

Organisation

- This is suitable as a whole-class activity

Resources

- PowerPoint presentation of science images, words and people

What to do

- Create a slideshow with lots of images relating to a particular topic. Divide the class into two or three teams.
- The first team must select a player who sits with their back to the screen. Their team members take it in turns to describe each image to the player without using the actual name of the person or object. For example:

  'This is a power source.'
  'Its other name is a cell.'
  'You would find it in a circuit.'
  'Is it a battery?'

- The player has up to ten seconds to guess before moving onto the next team member.

- When an image has been correctly identified, someone else from the team takes the seat. A point is scored for each correctly identified item/ person, etc.

- Teams play for a maximum of five minutes, after which time the other team has a turn.

- The team with the most points after its five minutes wins.

Variations

- Instead of one person guessing, have pairs of children so they can confer.
- If an image is guessed in the first go, then that scores ten points.
- Increase or decrease the time limit.

Battleships

Battleships is classic game perfectly suited to learning scientific terms and for improving vocabulary and spelling.

Suitable for

KS1
KS2

Aims

- To enrich vocabularies and improve understanding of scientific terms.
- To articulate, qualify and justify thinking.
- To strengthen connections between key concepts and ideas.
- To consider what sources of information they will use to answer questions.

Organisation

- This is suitable as a whole-class activity

Resources

- Battleship grids

What to do

- Children draw a 10 by 10 coordinate grid and take turns guessing coordinates that could reveal the individual letters of a science word.
- If a coordinate is guessed correctly, then the letter is revealed, and this is recorded on the grid.
- The person who asked the question gets another go if they guess one of the coordinates correctly.
- When someone has guessed all the coordinates of a ship/science word and can say the word, then five points are scored.
- An additional five points can be scored if a definition can be given.

Variations

- Use a smaller or larger grid.
- Hide more than one word on a grid.
- Use letters and numbers for the coordinates.
- Get children to invent a new scoring system.

Dungeon

Dungeon is based on an old fairy story about a rich queen who liked to play a game of probability with her people.

Suitable for

KS1
KS2

Aims

- To enrich vocabularies and improve understanding of scientific terms.
- To articulate, qualify and justify thinking.
- To strengthen connections between key concepts and ideas.
- To consider what sources of information they will use to answer questions.

Organisation

- This is suitable as a whole-class activity

Resources

- Pieces of A4 paper to act as steps
- A die labelled 1, 2, 3 and –1, –2 and –3

What to do

- Explain to the children that there was once a queen who liked to play a game with the people she ruled over.
- The queen had a staircase with 13 steps. There were six steps up to a bag of gold and six steps down to the dungeon, with one in the middle. Anyone who dared to play began on the middle step.
- The queen tossed a die with 1, 2, 3, –1, –2, –3 on it and the person would move up and down the staircase according to the number that the queen threw.

- Children play the game, with one volunteer playing the part of the queen and the others taking it in turns to 'move up and down the steps'.

Variations

- An adaptation of this game is for children to start on the middle step and answer a series of questions based on the topic just studied: the queen asks a question and if the answer is correct then the player moves up the stairs. If it is incorrect, then the player moves down the stairs. If a player reaches the top of the stairs then ten points are scored. If a player ends up in the dungeon then no points are scored.
- Change the number of steps to three steps up and five down.
- Have a danger step which means that if you fail to answer a question correctly you lose five points, as well as having to move back.
- Have a chance step which means you can swap your question for another if you don't know the answer to the one given.

Word dice

Word dice is a fun game for improving children's science vocabulary.

Suitable for

KS1
KS2

Aims

- To enrich vocabularies and improve understanding of scientific terms.
- To articulate, qualify and justify thinking.
- To strengthen connections between key concepts and ideas.
- To consider what sources of information they will use to answer questions.

Organisation

- This is suitable as a whole-class activity

Resources

- Access to the internet

What to do

- Go to the site www.crickweb.co.uk/assets/resources/flash. php?&file=worddice and enter six science words per die.
- Ask a volunteer to roll the die and, whatever word the die lands on, children have to provide a definition of that word.
- You could throw two dice so children have to use a sentence with both words in.

Variations

- You could play this with ordinary dice. Have a list of words prepared for the number 1, number 2 and so on up to 6. When someone throws a die, look at the number thrown and read out one of the words from your list next to that number.

- Instead of a word you could have letters of the alphabet equating to particular numbers: for example, 1 = a, b, c, d, e, f, g; 2 = h, i, j, k, and so on. Whatever number is thrown, players have to think of a science word beginning with that letter.

Science hangman

Science hangman is based on a classic game and is an ideal vocabulary builder for learning new words.

Suitable for

KS1
KS2

Aims

- To enrich vocabularies and improve understanding of scientific terms.
- To articulate, qualify and justify thinking.
- To strengthen connections between key concepts and ideas.
- To consider what sources of information they will use to answer questions.

Organisation

- This is suitable as a whole-class activity

Resources

- No special resources needed

What to do

- Think of an appropriate science word.
- Count the letters of this word and write down that number of spaces.
- Next draw an upside-down L.
- The class guess a letter and, if it is correct, you put it in the blank. If it is incorrect, you put a head on the upside-down L.
- Keep drawing body parts for each subsequent wrong guess.
- The object is for the children to guess the word before you complete the body.

Variations

- Children can play this game in small groups against each other.
- Have bonus points for the correct definition of a word.
- Have bonus points for three associated words.

Loop cards

Loop cards or key word chases are excellent ways of covering a lot of ground in a lesson and they help children learn associated facts quickly when used regularly.

Suitable for

KS1
KS2

Aims

- To enrich vocabularies and improve understanding of scientific terms.
- To articulate, qualify and justify thinking.
- To strengthen connections between key concepts and ideas.
- To consider what sources of information they will use to answer questions.

Organisation

- This is suitable as a whole-class activity

Resources

- Loop cards suitable for your year group, which can be downloaded from www.sheffield.gov.uk/?pgid=51541&fs=n

What to do

- Make a set of cards in relation to the topic you are studying.
- On one half of the card should be a question and on the other half an answer, but one that doesn't match the question.
- Give pairs of children a loop card each and ask them to read their question and to try and think of the answer.
- Starting with one pair, ask them to read out their question. If any other pair have the matching answer then they should say the answer. They then read out their question.

- This continues around the class until each pair has asked and answered a question.

Example loop cards:

Materials which can stand the heat of an oven are said to be ...	... 250 ˚C.
When heated, ovenproof materials will not ...	... ovenproof.
When we remove anything from an oven we need to use ...	... crack, melt or change.
Oven gloves are made from ...	... oven gloves.
If we cover an object to keep it warm or cold for longer ...	... insulating materials.
Materials which do not allow heat to pass easily are ...	... we insulate it.
Examples of thermal insulators include ...	... thermal insulators.
Materials which allow heat to pass easily are called ...	... wool, bubble wrap and fleece.
Examples of thermal conductors include ...	... thermal conductors.
Materials that are good thermal conductors are good for making ...	... aluminium, tin and steel.
The measure of heat energy, or how hot or cold something is ...	... saucepans and frying pans.

We measure temperature using ...	... temperature.
Temperature is measured in ...	... a thermometer.
The symbol for degrees Celsius is ...	... degrees Celsius.
The freezing point of water is ...	˚C.
The boiling point of water is ...	(zero) 0˚C.
The temperature of the human body is ...	... 100˚C.
Room temperature is ...	... about 37˚C.
The temperature of the inside of a fridge is ...	... about 20˚C.
The temperature of the inside of a freezer is ...	... about 4˚C.
We can use the same insulating materials to ...	... about minus 20˚C.
A hot drink if left will ...	... keep things warm or cold.
A cold drink if left will ...	... slowly cool down until it reaches room temperature.
When water cools to 0˚C it ...	... slowly warm up until it reaches room temperature.

When ice is warmed it ...	... freezes.
When water is boiled it ...	... melts.
When water vapour is cooled it ...	... evaporates.
We cook our food in ovens at temperatures up to ...	... condenses.

Variations

- Some pupils could hold more than one card.
- Increase or decrease the number of loop cards.

Taboo

Taboo is a word-guessing party game that really gets children thinking and helps build their science vocabulary.

Suitable for

KS1
KS2

Aims

- To enrich vocabularies and improve understanding of scientific terms.
- To articulate, qualify and justify thinking.
- To strengthen connections between key concepts and ideas.
- To consider what sources of information they will use to answer questions.

Organisation

- This is suitable for three players

Resources

- Taboo cards
- Word mats

What to do

- Ask children what the word 'taboo' means and then explain the rules of the game. One player has to give the definition of a word and describe it to player 2 without using a list of words that are taboo. Player 3 listens to make sure none of the taboo words is used.
- Players take it in turns to describe, guess and listen.
- Have a dummy run playing taboo using the following example: 'Give a definition for the word "conductor" without using the words heat, metal, electricity.'

- Now look at other taboo cards about electricity and let children try these for themselves.

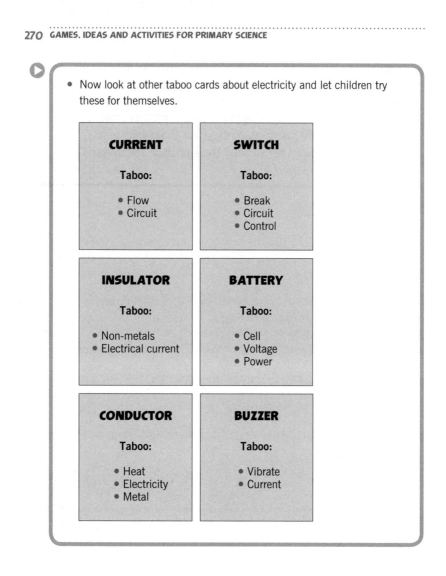

CURRENT

Taboo:

- Flow
- Circuit

SWITCH

Taboo:

- Break
- Circuit
- Control

INSULATOR

Taboo:

- Non-metals
- Electrical current

BATTERY

Taboo:

- Cell
- Voltage
- Power

CONDUCTOR

Taboo:

- Heat
- Electricity
- Metal

BUZZER

Taboo:

- Vibrate
- Current

Variations

- Taboo can be used to study or revise any topic. Ideas for materials include the following:

WOOL	**WOOD**	**GLASS**	**PLASTIC**	**METAL**
Taboo:	Taboo:	Taboo:	Taboo:	Taboo:
• Sheep • Jumper • Knitting	• Tree • Building	• Window • Bottle • Sand	• Toys • Bag • Sandwich box	• Magnetic • Shiny

- Use more taboo words on the card to make the game more difficult. For example:

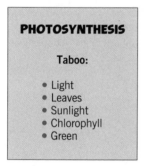

PHOTOSYNTHESIS

Taboo:

- Light
- Leaves
- Sunlight
- Chlorophyll
- Green

- Allow children to use word mats if they need help thinking of a word.
- Print taboo words on the front and back of cards.
- Use pictures instead of words.

Verbal tennis

Verbal tennis is a word association game that gets children thinking on their feet.

Suitable for

KS1
KS2

Aims

- To enrich vocabularies and improve understanding of scientific terms.
- To articulate, qualify and justify thinking.
- To strengthen connections between key concepts and ideas.
- To consider what sources of information they will use to answer questions.

Organisation

- This is suitable for two or three players

Resources

- No special resources needed

What to do

- Children sit in pairs, facing each other.
- Decide on a topic and the pair decides who will 'serve' first.
- The server says a word or phrase associated with the topic and the partner must immediately respond with a second word or phrase.
- Play continues until a player hesitates, makes a mistake, repeats a word/phrase that has already been used or is inaccurate.
- Scoring follows the rules of tennis and points are scored as 15–0, 15–15, etc.

- For example, on the subject of light, an exchange might go something like this:

  Player 1: candle
  Player 2: sun
  Player 1: shadow
  Player 2: absorb
  Player 1: scatter
  Player 2: reflect
  Player 1:

Variations

- Another way to play this is to have three players so that they play in a triangle. Rather than choosing a specific topic, players select a letter of the alphabet and have to think of as many science-related words as they can beginning with that letter. For example:

  C
  Player 1: canine
  Player 2: calcium
  Player 3: carbon dioxide
  Player 1: circuit
  Player 2: Celsius
  Player 3: concave
  Player 1: convex
  Player 2: clay
  Player 3: chlorophyll
  Player 1: circulatory system
  Player 2:
  Player 3:

- Use a different scoring system.
- Increase the number of players and have a taboo competition.

Bingo

> Bingo is an interactive game designed to help children improve their word definitions and science vocabulary.

Suitable for

KS1
KS2

Aims

- To enrich vocabularies and improve understanding of scientific terms.
- To articulate, qualify and justify thinking.
- To strengthen connections between key concepts and ideas.
- To consider what sources of information they will use to answer questions.

Organisation

- This is suitable for the whole class

Resources

- No special resources needed

What to do

- Write some key words from the topic you are studying on the board. For example: changing sounds: decibels, ear canal, ear drum, frequency, high pitch, low pitch, muffle, note, percussion instruments, pitch, sound insulator, sound source, sound waves, string instruments, tension, tuning, vibration, volume, wind instruments.
- Now get children to draw a grid with nine squares and fill them with nine of the terms and words you have written on the board.

- Tell children that you will read out the definitions relating to those key words and concepts. If children can match your definition to a word on their grid then they cross the word off.
- The winner is the first player to cross off all their words and call 'Bingo!'

Variations

- Increase the size of the grid you are playing with.
- The winner could be the first person to cross off their words in a column or a diagonal.

Just a science minute

Just a science minute is based on the radio game in which players talk for 60 seconds on a given subject. This can be used in science to recap a lesson and see how much has been learnt or to use a novel way of revising content of a topic.

Suitable for

KS1
KS2

Aims

- To enrich vocabularies and improve understanding of scientific terms.
- To articulate, qualify and justify thinking.
- To strengthen connections between key concepts and ideas.
- To consider what sources of information they will use to answer questions.

Organisation

- This is suitable as a whole-class activity

Resources

- Timer/stopwatch

What to do

- Explain the rules to children: that someone is challenged to speak for 60 seconds on a science topic or experiment without repetition, hesitation or deviation.
- Explain that repetition means that key words cannot be used more than once, hesitation means no pausing and deviation means not going off the subject.

- Tell children that they can challenge someone if they think they have repeated a word, hesitated or deviated.
- If you think the challenge is fair, then the challenger takes over the topic and tries to talk for the remaining time.

Variations

- You might choose to change the rules so that someone is challenged to talk for a minute about the lesson without hesitating.
- Increase or decrease the time limit.

Mastermind

Mastermind is the science version of the quiz show which tests contestants' specialist and general knowledge skills.

Suitable for

KS1
KS2

Aims

- To enrich vocabularies and improve understanding of scientific terms.
- To articulate, qualify and justify thinking.
- To strengthen connections between key concepts and ideas.
- To consider what sources of information they will use to answer questions.

Organisation

- This is suitable for groups of four or as whole-class activity

Resources

- Timer/stopwatch

What to do

- Set up a Mastermind competition based on the format of the TV programme. There are two rounds. In round one children answer questions on their science specialist subject for one minute.
- Round two is general revision questions from the topic.
- Different children can have different specialist subjects and compete in a group of four to decide the winner.
- Give children advance warning so that they can revise their specialist subject and the topic in general.

Variations

- Children can play as a group to answer questions rather than individually.
- A different time limit can be given.
- Use the music from the actual *Mastermind* show and ask children to talk about how it makes them feel.

Pictionary

Pictionary is a picture-based word-guessing game that is a lot of fun to play within the context of any science topic.

Suitable for

KS1
KS2

Aims

- To enrich vocabularies and improve understanding of scientific terms.
- To articulate, qualify and justify thinking.
- To strengthen connections between key concepts and ideas
- To consider what sources of information they will use to answer questions.

Organisation

- This is suitable as a whole-class activity

Resources

- Science word mats and dictionaries

What to do

- Cut up some key words, concepts and terms from a word mat or dictionary and place them in a hat.
- Divide the class up into teams.
- Each team member takes it in turns to pick a word out of a hat and must produce a picture of what is on the card on the class whiteboard.
- Allow 60 seconds for drawing the image. The rules are no talking, miming, or writing words.
- Team members have to guess what the image is. Score five points for a correct guess. If a word cannot be guessed then no points are scored.

Variations

- Players can play to a time limit of 30 seconds.
- Players pair up from the same team and draw the word together.
- One player from one team and another player from the other team play at the same time, drawing different words on the class whiteboard.
- Children can play in small groups rather than as a class.
- This activity could be acted out instead of, or as well as, drawing. The action can involve facial expression, gesture and props. The first player to guess the word then acts out a new word. Try playing this for words such as: food chain, gravity, sound waves, melting, pollination, evaporation, magnetism, insoluble, separation, air resistance and so on.

Wonder words

This is a science word-building game, similar to the game Boggle, and can be played to build science vocabulary.

Suitable for

KS1
KS2

Aims

- To enrich vocabularies and improve understanding of scientific terms.
- To articulate, qualify and justify thinking.
- To strengthen connections between key concepts and ideas.
- To consider what sources of information they will use to answer questions.

Organisation

- This is suitable as a whole-class activity

Resources

- Science word mats and dictionaries
- Letter dice

What to do

- The idea of this game is for children to think of as many science words as possible from a given number of letters.
- Each player draws a 5 x 6 grid of squares.
- Ask a volunteer to think of a letter.
- Everyone writes this letter in any of their squares.
- Go around the class asking everyone for a letter – everyone writes the letter called out into any of their squares.

- When all the squares have been filled in, children are given five minutes to combine letters together to make a science word.
- A scoring system can be worked out according to the number of words created, or for words that contain a certain number of letters.

Variations

- Use a set of letter dice to generate the letters.
- The game can be played so that children have to write a science word beginning with the letter written in each box.

Word link

Word link is a challenging game for improving knowledge and understanding of key scientific words and terms.

Suitable for

KS1
KS2

Aims

- To enrich vocabularies and improve understanding of scientific terms.
- To articulate, qualify and justify thinking.
- To strengthen connections between key concepts and ideas.
- To consider what sources of information they will use to answer questions.

Organisation

- This is suitable as a whole-class activity

Resources

- Science word mats and dictionaries

What to do

- Word link involves selecting a science word and then writing it down the left-hand side of a grid and writing it backwards down the right-hand side of the grid. An example is given on page 285.

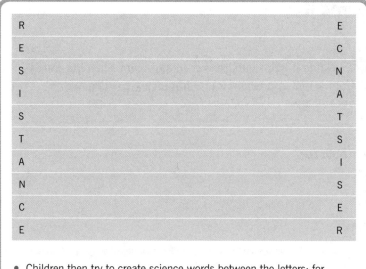

R	E
E	C
S	N
I	A
S	T
T	S
A	I
N	S
C	E
E	R

- Children then try to create science words between the letters: for example, a word beginning in r and ending in e (other than resistance), such as 'residue'.

- Some letters will be more difficult than others to make into a word, and for some it might be impossible, but the game gets children thinking about and talking about science.

Variation

- Rather than choosing a science word as the starting point, you could choose any word at all but the words in between have to be science related.

Name it

Name it helps children recall and learn scientific words from A to Z and is perfect for improving spelling and vocabulary.

Suitable for

KS1
KS2

Aims

- To enrich vocabularies and improve understanding of scientific terms.
- To articulate, qualify and justify thinking.
- To strengthen connections between key concepts and ideas.
- To consider what sources of information they will use to answer questions.

Organisation

- This is suitable as a whole-class activity

Resources

- Science word mats and dictionaries

What to do

- Name it involves writing a name down the side of a piece of paper. This doesn't have to be a science name – you can choose someone's name in the class. It is better if you can choose someone with a name in which no letter is repeated more than once.

- Players then have five minutes to think of as many science-related words as possible beginning with each letter of the name. For example:

    A acid, alkali, allergy, atoms
    N Newton, nitrogen
    D decomposition
    R radar, respiration
    E electricity, evaporation
    W water, weight

- The winner is the person with the most words.

Variations

- You can award one point per word and award bonus points if a letter has five words next to it.
- Children could choose two letters and combine the words they have thought of to write a sentence, paragraph or short story.

Countdown

Countdown uses the TV show as inspiration for using anagrams to improve word-building skills.

Suitable for

KS1
KS2

Aims

- To enrich vocabularies and improve understanding of scientific terms.
- To articulate, qualify and justify thinking.
- To strengthen connections between key concepts and ideas.
- To consider what sources of information they will use to answer questions.

Organisation

- This is suitable as a whole-class activity

Resources

- Science word mats and dictionaries

What to do

- Show children the following anagram and ask them to unscramble the letters to make a scientific word: unit solo (solution).
- Provide children with clues to help them as necessary.
- Write more anagrams on the board for children to solve. For example:

    shoe hypnotists (photosynthesis)
    pea mutterer (temperature)
    earth bio inn (hibernation)
    daycare broth (carbohydrate)

unloads rust (ultrasounds)

moon-starers (astronomers)

- The first child to get all the anagrams wins.
- Now provide children with a word list of science words you want them to learn and ask them to make up some of their own anagrams for them.

Variations

- Children can work in small groups to solve the anagrams.
- You can theme anagrams or include a mixed bag. Here are some related to animals:

  hush of nice (house finch)

  a pencil (pelican)

  organ oak (kangaroo)

  pine gun (penguin)

- Impose a time limit for each anagram and set this to music. You can download the *Countdown* music and have a timer to add to the drama too (see classtools.net/education-games-php/timer/)

Kim's game

Kim's game is a memory game and can be used for helping children name and remember resources related to an investigation or enquiry.

Suitable for

KS1
KS2

Aims

- To enrich vocabularies and improve understanding of scientific terms.
- To articulate, qualify and justify thinking.
- To strengthen connections between key concepts and ideas.
- To consider what sources of information they will use to answer questions.

Organisation

- This is suitable as a whole-class activity.

Resources

- Various pieces of equipment and apparatus related to an experiment or demonstration

What to do

- Place some objects on a tray or table (for example, the equipment needed for a particular experiment) and cover it over with a large cloth.
- Show the objects to the class for one minute and then cover them again. Children then have to write down as many objects as they can remember.

- The person who remembers the most objects wins the game.
- Now go through the objects, naming them and discussing what they are made of and used for.

Variations

- Show various objects on the class whiteboard to make things easier to see.
- This is a good game to play before an investigation without saying what the investigation will be about. For example, show children the objects below and then challenge them to say what the bits and pieces might be used for.

  A pair of scissors
  Sellotape
  A piece of card
  Eight plastic straws
  A ruler
  A piece of card
  A tape recorder

Football

Football is a fun game that can be played to make revision more interesting.

Suitable for

KS1
KS2

Aims

- To enrich vocabularies and improve understanding of scientific terms.
- To articulate, qualify and justify thinking.
- To strengthen connections between key concepts and ideas.
- To consider what sources of information they will use to answer questions.

Organisation

- This is suitable for the whole class playing in two teams.

Resources

- Football pitch and score card printed onto card or drawn onto a whiteboard
- Dice
- Coloured counter

What to do

- Divide the class into two teams and draw a football pitch and scorecard on the board as follows:

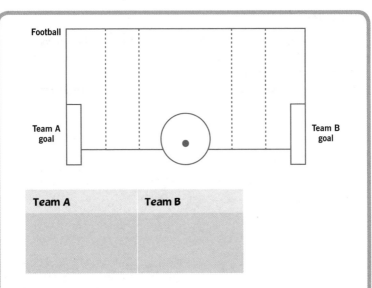

Football

Team A goal

Team B goal

Team A	Team B

- The counter should be placed at the centre of the pitch. Roll a die to decide which team goes first (lowest number starts).

- Questions are asked of each team in turn on any topic or a specific theme.

- Teams confer, then give their answer. If the answer is correct, they can move the counter one space towards their opponent's goal. This means moving forward to the next part of the pitch. The team keeps possession of 'the ball' and gets another go.

- If the answer is incorrect, the other team takes possession of 'the ball' and it's now their turn to answer a question. If they answer correctly, the ball moves one space in the opposite direction and they get another go. If they answer incorrectly, the other team takes possession.

- Each team aims to reach their opponents' goal.

- Decide when the game should end, either according to a time limit or when one team scores, say, three goals.

Variations

- Play this game as 'beat the teacher' where the class play against you.
- After a goal is scored, have the scoring team 'kick off' first rather than the team conceding the goal.
- If a team scores a goal, they can add another goal to their tally by spelling a word correctly.

Dragons' Den

Dragons' Den is a science version of the TV show. Children take on the role of a famous scientist and pitch ideas to pretend entrepreneurs.

Suitable for

KS1
KS2

Aims

- To enrich vocabularies and improve understanding of scientific terms.
- To articulate, qualify and justify thinking.
- To strengthen connections between key concepts and ideas.
- To consider what sources of information they will use to answer questions.

Organisation

- This is suitable for small groups of two to four.

Resources

- Reference books and internet access

What to do

- Show children a clip of *Dragons' Den* if they have never seen the show before.
- Get children to imagine that they are an inventor trying to persuade 'the Dragons' to invest in their product.
- This could be an invention from the past, such as the telephone or light bulb, or something they have thought of themselves.

- Children can write the dialogue in small groups and act it out in the style of the TV programme. For example, Leonardo da Vinci might walk up the stairs and present himself as follows:

'Hello, Dragons, my name is Leonardo da Vinci and I'm the Managing Director of da Vinci's. I'm here to tell you about my new invention called the parachute and I'm asking for £100 for a 10 per cent stake in my business.

'The parachute is a device which will help people jump safely from burning buildings. My design consists of a linen cloth held together by a pyramid of wooden poles about seven metres long. I have a sketch here if you would like to have a look. Are there any questions?'

Dragon 1: Hi Leonardo, I'm Theo. Have you tested it?
Leonardo: No, but I am confident it works. I've got a few working models to show you. One is the tent design but I've also got a couple of other prototypes that are circular.
Dragon 1: So, you want £100 for something we don't actually know will work? I can't invest in something that hasn't been tried and tested and for that reason I'm out.
Dragon 2: Hi Leonardo, I'm Deborah. Leonardo, how many have you sold?
Leonardo: I've sold three so far.
Dragon 2: And how much do they retail for?
Leonardo: I'm selling them for £9.99.
Dragon 2: Do you know, I like this product but I'm not sure whether there is a market for it. You basically need tall buildings to burn for it to be useful.
Leonardo: It's a safety device and it's there for people to have should the worst happen.

- The idea is that children research what they can about Leonardo da Vinci's parachute and create dialogue around it. This would also be the opportunity for children to demonstrate parachutes they have made out of various materials to show how they work and which designs are the most effective. Most likely this invention would have been thrown out by the Dragons but it is easy to see how some ideas might have initially appeared fantastical and foolhardy, yet have become part of daily life and accepted as indispensable today.

Variations

- Invite other teachers to act as the Dragons.
- Use this idea as part of an assembly.
- Children could write the dialogue by personifying the product so that it speaks and tells the Dragons what it can do.

Dominoes

Dominoes is an excellent game for helping children learn unfamiliar terms, phrases and expressions.

Suitable for

KS1
KS2

Aims

- To enrich vocabularies and improve understanding of scientific terms.
- To articulate, qualify and justify thinking.
- To strengthen connections between key concepts and ideas.
- To consider what sources of information they will use to answer questions.

Organisation

- This is suitable for two players.

Resources

- Domino templates

What to do

- Explain how to play dominoes for any children who are unsure.
- The first player places one of their dominoes (right-side up) on the table. The second player tries to put a domino on the table that matches one side of what is already there.
- If a player cannot go, the player picks a domino from the pile and skips that turn.
- Children continue taking turns putting dominoes on the board (or picking one from the pile if they cannot go) until someone wins.
- The winner is the first person to get rid of all of their dominoes.

- If no one can go, then the person with the fewest dominos left is the winner.
- Here is an example of a science domino game:

Petal	They protect the flower while it is still a bud.
Sepal	This is where the flower makes nectar. These are usually right in the centre of the flower.
Nectaries	The female part of the flower where seeds are made.
Carpel	These are the male parts of the flower. They make pollen.
Ovary	Bees and other insects 'collect' pollen from here and travel to other plants and 'drop' it on the stigma of other plants.

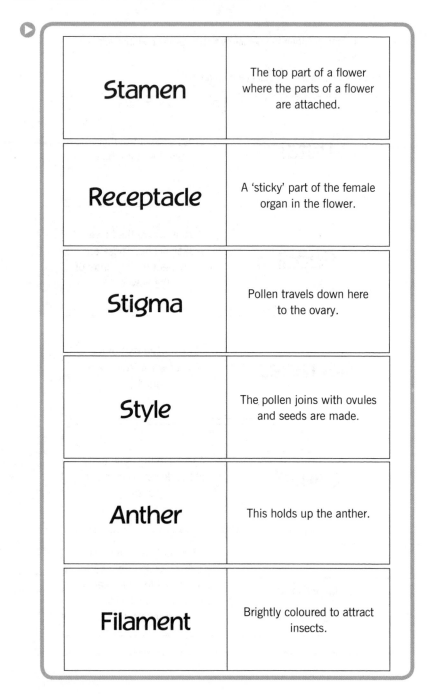

Stamen	The top part of a flower where the parts of a flower are attached.
Receptacle	A 'sticky' part of the female organ in the flower.
Stigma	Pollen travels down here to the ovary.
Style	The pollen joins with ovules and seeds are made.
Anther	This holds up the anther.
Filament	Brightly coloured to attract insects.

Variations

- You could include blank dominoes to act as 'any word' cards.
- Children could be challenged to create their own set of dominoes.

Quiz, quiz, trade

Quiz, quiz, trade is a highly effective game for learning topic material and getting to grips with new content.

Suitable for

KS1
KS2

Aims

- To enrich vocabularies and improve understanding of scientific terms.
- To articulate, qualify and justify thinking.
- To strengthen connections between key concepts and ideas.
- To consider what sources of information they will use to answer questions.

Organisation

- This is suitable as a whole-class activity

Resources

- Quiz, quiz, trade cards

What to do

- Each child should be given a card with a question on one side and the answer to the question on the opposite side of the card, or the question and answer on both sides of the same card.
- Children should get out of their seats, partner up and quiz each other.
- Once a player gets the correct answer, players switch partners and trade cards.

Question: What do we call the lines of force surrounding a magnet?

A Magnetic pasture
B Magnetic field
C Magnetic dale

Answer: B

Question: Iron filings can be used to help you see the field lines around a magnet.

A True
B False

Answer: A

Question: A small magnet that will point to the North Pole of the Earth is called a ...?

A Clock
B Compass
C Computer

Answer: B

Question: The magnetic field is strongest near the poles of a magnet.

A True
B False

Answer: A

Question: What word is used to describe magnets moving closer together due to a magnetic force?

A Attraction
B Repulsion
C Opposition

Answer: A

Question: What is magnetism?

Answer: Magnetism is a force created by electricity.

Question: What are electromagnets?

Answer: Electromagnets are produced by placing a metal core inside a coil of wire carrying an electric current.

Question: What do we call the ends of a magnet?

A bars
B sticks
C poles

Answer: C

Question: Which materials are attracted by magnets?

Answer: Iron and steel.

Question: In which direction will a pivoted magnet point?

Answer: North–south.

Question: When two North poles of a magnet are put together, what happens?

Answer: They repel.

Question: When the North and South poles of a magnet are put together, what happens?

Answer: They attract.

Question: What is meant by the word 'attract'?

Answer: To move together.

Question: When two South poles of a magnet are put together what happens?

Answer: They repel.

Question: What do unlike poles of a magnet do?

Answer: They attract.

Question: What happens if you hang a bar magnet from a thread?

Answer: It will come to rest in a direction facing north–south.

Question: What happens if you place a magnet alongside a non-magnetised steel knitting needle?

Answer: After some time it will magnetise it.

Question: What is meant by the word 'repel'?

Answer: To push away.

Question: What causes the Earth's magnetic field?

Answer: The Earth's liquid core sloshing around as it spins.

Question: What happens when a magnet is put near a copper bracelet?

Answer: Copper is non-magnetic so nothing will happen.

Question: What are magnetic tool bar tools made of?

Answer: Iron or steel.

Question: What are naturally occurring magnets in nature called?

Answer: Lodestones.

Question: What happens if you stroke a piece of unmagnetised iron or steel with a known magnet?

Answer: It can make it into a magnet.

Question: How can a magnet be destroyed?

Answer: By dropping it or hammering it and by heating it.

Question: What happens when magnets are broken into small bits?

Answer: The bits themselves become small magnets.

Variations

- Get children to create their own cards for another class to try.
- Change the level of complexity as needed.
- Children could play in pairs rather than individually.

I spy

I spy is another classic game that can be adapted for the science classroom. This guessing game helps children improve their observational skills by searching their environment for objects.

Suitable for

KS1
KS2

Aims

- To enrich vocabularies and improve understanding of scientific terms.
- To articulate, qualify and justify thinking.
- To strengthen connections between key concepts and ideas.
- To consider what sources of information they will use to answer questions.

Organisation

- This is suitable as a whole-class activity.

Resources

- No special resources needed

What to do

- There are a couple of ways of playing the game. One way is to choose a topic and focus on getting children to hunt for objects that match your chosen letter. The obvious area to concentrate on is materials: for example, 'I spy with my little eye something beginning with P.' You could restrict this to just one item or include many. So something beginning with P could be pencil, paper, plastic, polystyrene, polythene, polyester, perspex, etc.

- Another way to approach this game is to avoid using a letter but be specific in terms of a characteristic. For example: I spy ...

  ... something that is transparent.
  ... something that is a producer.
  ... something that has energy.
  ... something that is evaporating.
  ... something that is waterproof.
  ... something that is magnetic.
  ... something that is an insulator.
  ... something that is breathing.
  ... something that is absorbent.
  ... something that is soluble.
  ... something that is reflective.
  ... something that is brittle.
  ... something that has a shadow.
  ... something that is part of a food chain.
  ... something that is used to measure a force.
  ... something that needs electricity to produce movement.
  ... something that always keeps the same shape.
  ... something that has got a shell.

Variation

- A further variation of the game is 'I hear with my little ear', which concentrates on sounds instead of sights.

Categories

Categories is a word game in which players think of words that begin with specified letters and that belong to specified categories.

Suitable for

KS1
KS2

Aims

- To enrich vocabularies and improve understanding of scientific terms.
- To articulate, qualify and justify thinking.
- To strengthen connections between key concepts and ideas.
- To consider what sources of information they will use to answer questions.

Organisation

- This is suitable as a whole-class activity

Resources

- No special resources needed

What to do

- Draw a 5 x 6 grid.
- Now choose four initial letters and five categories; these become the column and row headings of the grid respectively.
- Next challenge children to fill the grid within ten minutes using the column headings as the first letters of various words that relate to the subjects in the row headings. For example:

Categories	Round one letter: M	Round two letter: O	Round three letter: D	Round four letter: P
teeth			decay	
magnets		opposite		
materials	match			particles
rocks				
light		opaque		

Variations

- You could include more categories or more letters.
- You could present a completed grid that contains deliberate mistakes for children to spot.

Science shop

Science shop tests children's knowledge of scientific words and helps to build their bank of terms and concepts.

Suitable for

KS1
KS2

Aims

- To enrich vocabularies and improve understanding of scientific terms.
- To articulate, qualify and justify thinking.
- To strengthen connections between key concepts and ideas.
- To consider what sources of information they will use to answer questions.

Organisation

- This is suitable as a whole-class activity

Resources

- No special resources needed

What to do

- Explain that the game involves each child in turn saying something that they bought in a fictitious science shop.
- The rule is that the science word given has to begin with the last letter of the word said previously.
- If one child starts by saying 'shadow' then the next has to use the last letter and begin a new word: for example, 'wave'. The following player has to think of a word beginning with 'e': for example, echo.

- The idea is to move around the class, but whatever items have been listed previously have to be repeated: for example, 'I went to the science shop and I bought a shadow, a wave, an echo and some oxygen.' The game gets more difficult as it progresses.

Variations

- Another game to play is 'I packed my science bag'. This is similar to science shop, but doesn't impose the rule of 'last letter and first letter' so there is more freedom. The idea is to go around the class and repeat what everyone else has said before you. For example:

  'I packed my science bag and in it I put some gravity.'
  'I packed my science bag and in it I put some gravity and an ecosystem.'
  'I packed my science bag and in it I put some gravity, an ecosystem and a femur.'
  'I packed my science bag and in it I put some gravity, an ecosystem, a femur and a reversible change.'
  'I packed my science bag and in it I put some gravity, an ecosystem, a femur, a reversible change and a circuit.'
  'I packed my science bag and in it I put some gravity, an ecosystem, a femur, a reversible change, a circuit and a micro-organism.'
  'I packed my science bag and in it I put some gravity, an ecosystem, a femur, a reversible change, a circuit, a micro-organism and a stamen.'
  'I packed my science bag and in it I put some gravity, an ecosystem, a femur, a reversible change, a circuit, a micro-organism, a stamen and a clay particle.'
  'I packed my science bag and in it I put some gravity, an ecosystem, a femur, a reversible change, a circuit, a micro-organism, a stamen, a clay particle and a line graph.'

- If you want children to be challenged, ask them to add an adjective to describe everything they are putting in their bag: for example, a fractured femur, faulty circuit, etc. If they struggle, children can help each other with actions but not words.
- A common variation of the game is that the items listed must be in alphabetical order, so the first person would need to choose an object beginning with A, the second person's object would begin with B, and so on.

Wheel of fortune

Wheel of fortune is a fun way of testing science knowledge of a particular topic. It is great for summarising a topic or revision.

Suitable for

KS1
KS2

Aims

- To enrich vocabularies and improve understanding of scientific terms.
- To articulate, qualify and justify thinking.
- To strengthen connections between key concepts and ideas.
- To consider what sources of information they will use to answer questions.

Organisation

- This is suitable for small groups of two to four

Resources

- A spinner with eight sections. See www.murray.k12.ga.us/teacher/kara%20 leonard/Mini%20T's/Games/wheel.ppt

What to do

- Children play in small teams and create between them eight questions (and answers).
- Using an interactive whiteboard spinner with eight sections, one team starts by clicking the spin button.
- The number that the spinner lands on is the number the team look at on their list of questions. They then select another team to answer this question.

Variation

- Another version of this game is called In a spin. For this activity you will need a number spinner labelled up to 20. Arrange the class into a circle and place the spinner in the middle of the floor with 12 numbered cards spread around it (on the back of the cards are pictures, diagrams or questions related to the topic being studied). One child spins the wheel to generate a number. This player then turns over the card that matches the number on the wheel and attempts to answer the question. Points are given for each correct answer.

Chapter 7
Science and literacy activities

'The sun gives off light.
Therefore, the sun gives off feathers.'

Introduction

In this chapter you will find a collection of ideas for writing, speaking and listening. They can be used to enrich teaching and learning within science and literacy, and aim to connect the two in fun, creative and meaningful ways. Use the ideas here as regular activities either with the whole class or for group work while other classroom activities take place. They also make ideal activities for extending children and so can be used for challenges or for homework assignments.

Personification

> Personification challenges children to use their writing skills to give an inanimate object or concept human qualities. It is a fun way to bring science terms and ideas to life.

Suitable for

KS1
KS2

Aims

- To choose form and content to suit a particular purpose.
- To use and adapt the features of a form of writing.
- To review own work and the work of others and describe its significance and its limitations.
- To use writing to help thinking, investigating, organising and learning.

Organisation

- This is suitable for small groups of two to four

Resources

- No special resources required

What to do

- Ask children to think about describing an investigation or process from the point of view of one of the variables or objects involved.
- Invite pairs of children to give an account in their own words, using scientific vocabulary accurately and in context.
- This can be done either verbally or as a narrative, or both.
- In the example on page 318, the water cycle comes alive from the point of view of a raindrop and is told as a story.

My life as a raindrop:

What a day it's been! I started off in a cloud. There I was, minding my own business, just enjoying the view, when I bumped into a few of the other guys. When us droplets get together we make bigger droplets. Soon I am so heavy that my cloud can no longer hold me and gravity pulls me toward the Earth. I start to fall, bumping into smaller droplets and becoming even larger. I fall pretty quickly to Earth and, boy, what a ride that is! It's so exciting because there are thousands of us dive-bombing towards the big rock at the same time. We all love this part because we get to go so fast. Your scientists call this precipitation. It's worth pointing out that we don't fall just as raindrops but sometimes as hail, sleet and snow. Part of the precipitation thrill is not knowing where I'm going to land. Last week I landed on the windscreen of the Number 15 bus travelling down Oxford Street in London. I got hit by a windscreen wiper and landed in the gutter. Once I landed in the Atlantic Ocean and was there for weeks, and on another occasion I dropped straight on a lady's head just coming out of the hairdresser's. She wasn't happy but it wasn't my fault.

Anyway, where I land is pretty important because that decides what happens to me next. Drains are the worst. Take it from me, a sewer is the last place you want to be on a rainy day. Anyway, nothing like that today, thank the heavens. No, today I actually landed in a puddle outside a library. I must have been in the puddle for about three hours, just watching people coming and going with their books, but I soon evaporated when the Sun came out. Those Sun rays are really hot. This is the bit where I turn from a liquid into a gas. Now you see me, now you don't. It's at this point I like to call myself water vapour. This is my levitation trick really, the bit where I climb magically back up to the sky again. Some of my friends get really steamed up by this.

As I get higher and higher I also get colder and colder until I change back to a liquid again. So do my friends. We call this condensation and it's back to being in a cloud and the whole cycle starts again. Round and round we go. I wonder where I'll end up today?

- When children have read through their stories, let them read their drafts to a friend.
- From here a friend can feedback with two stars and a wish and ask any questions.
- After some editing, the story should be ready for a whole-class reading.

Variations

- Rather than a story, children could write a sentence or paragraph.
- The concept brought to life could be 'interviewed' for a radio or TV show.

Chin waggers

Chin waggers encourages children to write about a scientific process or idea by writing a conversation between two or more concepts or ideas.

Suitable for

KS1
KS2

Aims

- To use character, action and narrative to convey story, themes, emotions and ideas in plays they devise and script.
- To choose form and content to suit a particular purpose.
- To use and adapt the features of a form of writing.
- To review own work and the work of others and describe its significance and its limitations.
- To use writing to help thinking, investigating, organising and learning.

Organisation

- This is suitable for small groups of two to four

Resources

- No special resources needed

What to do

- Tell children that the aim of the lesson is to write a script from the point of view of a character or an object linked to a topic of their choice. For example, it could be the journey of blood around the body, components in a circuit talking to each other, the diary of a seed and so on. Children will need to decide whether they need pictures with their stories.

- To demonstrate, provide an example of two seeds talking together about growing up:

    Seed 1: I heard a rumour that us seeds will grow a lot quicker if we are given plenty of water.

    Seed 2: Not too much water though, because we'll drown.

    Seed 1: It might make a difference what type of water we are given. Sometimes we don't get a choice. I mean, rainwater isn't good for us is it, especially acid rain?

    Seed 2: I think mineral water is the best for us. Think about all the goodness it contains.

    Seed 1: We could try using orange juice or something and see how we grow with that.

    Seed 2: Yeah, I tell you what, I'll try cola for a week and you try tea for a week. Let's see who grows the most.

- Let children continue this 'chin wag' between seeds, or they can come up with their own ideas.

- Share ideas as a class.

- Let other groups listen to or look at each other's stories and allow time for feedback using two stars and a wish.

- Children should give their scripts a suitable title and add characters to develop ideas further.

Variations

- Act out the script in front of the class, or use as part of an assembly.
- Rather than a script, children could write a story or a diary entry.

Crazy science

Crazy science is an opportunity for children to go surreal and combine words and concepts to create silly science sentences.

Suitable for

KS1
KS2

Aims

- To use character, action and narrative to convey story, themes, emotions and ideas in plays they devise and script.
- To choose form and content to suit a particular purpose.
- To use and adapt the features of a form of writing.
- To review own work and the work of others and describe its significance and its limitations.
- To use writing to help thinking, investigating, organising and learning.

Organisation

- This is suitable for small groups of two to four

Resources

- Word mats and vocabulary lists

What to do

- Explain that in this activity you are looking for creative and funny sentences that are out of the ordinary.
- Say that these can be themed according to a topic or made into a random list. The sentences all start with 'I wish I was ...'
- For example: I wish I was the plaque on a camel's canines; I wish I was a cracked mirror inside a purple periscope.

- Give children time to think of their own silly sentence to add to your list.
- Ask for examples and write them on the board.
- Pair children up to create some joint efforts and add these to the list. For example: I wish I was ...

    ... a defective bulb in a parallel circuit.

    ... a micro-organism multiplying on someone's hand.

    ... a caterpillar in a broken food chain.

    ... a disc magnet that had dropped on the floor.

    ... some sand being heated in an oven.

    ... a chicken bone in a jar of vinegar.

    ... gravity attracting lots of trouble.

    ... a leather car being chased by a cow.

    ... a bicep contracting in a Mr Universe competition.

    ... the vibrating skin on an angry kettle drum.

    ... a stopwatch measuring the 100 m world record.

    ... a colander separating peas at tea time.

    ... a dandelion seed being blown away by the wind.

    ... a sound wave travelling through a swimming pool of jelly.

    ... a variable that was out of control.

    ... a heartbeat just taking a rest.

Variations

- Children could perform their silly sentences in front of the class.
- Children could imagine that their wish had come true and describe what it was like.
- Children could choose a sentence and turn it into a headline or a story.

Alphabet science

Alphabet science makes a great warm-up and helps improve scientific vocabulary word building.

Suitable for

KS1
KS2

Aims

- To use character, action and narrative to convey story, themes, emotions and ideas in plays they devise and script.
- To choose form and content to suit a particular purpose.
- To use and adapt the features of a form of writing.
- To review own work and the work of others and describe its significance and its limitations.
- To use writing to help thinking, investigating, organising and learning.

Organisation

- This is suitable for small groups of two to four

Resources

- 'Wow words' word mats, vocabulary lists and science dictionaries

What to do

- Ask children to choose a name and a scientific object or concept with the same first letter, then connect them together with a suitable verb.
- They can add an adjective to describe the object or concept to make it more interesting.

- They can also include a preposition within the sentence. These can be a mixture of alliterative sentences and non-alliterative sentences. For example:

    Ani meditated with an absent-minded amphibian.
    Balroop bumped into a bewildered battery.
    Caitlin entertained a cautious conductor.
    Dexter frightened a delicate digestive system.
    Ena hovered above an eccentric elbow.
    Fiona prayed inside a friendly filter funnel.
    Gary gazed at a gregarious gravitational field.
    Heidi helped a hapless hypothesis.

Variations

- Ask children to focus on one letter of the alphabet and write a series of sentences: for example, four sentences for each letter.
- Children could write a news report to go with one of the sentences.

Faulty sentences

Faulty sentences asks children to work in pairs to create and correct science sentences that are faulty in some way.

Suitable for

KS1
KS2

Aims

- To use character, action and narrative to convey story, themes, emotions and ideas in plays they devise and script.
- To choose form and content to suit a particular purpose.
- To use and adapt the features of a form of writing.
- To review own work and the work of others and describe its significance and its limitations.
- To use writing to help thinking, investigating, organising and learning.

Organisation

- This is suitable for small groups of two to four

Resources

- Vocabulary lists and science dictionaries
- Access to the internet

What to do

- Explain to children that you have collected together some sentences from a science book which you think are wrong in some way.
- Say that the sentences need completely revising or adapting to make them more accurate: for example, 'Gravity is a force that pulls us upwards.'

- Children will have no problem spotting that the faulty word is 'upwards' and that it needs replacing with 'downwards'. Here are some more examples for children to try:

    Like poles will attract and unlike poles repel.
    Tight strings on a guitar will make a low-pitched sound.
    Stretching a spring makes it smaller.
    Foil is an excellent sound insulator.
    Touching a battery is dangerous.
    If you look on the back of a spoon your face is upside down.

- After working through and discussing the examples, children can invent their own.

Variation

- Children could write a letter of complaint to a publisher, pointing out its faulty sentences.

Science newsflash

Science newsflash involves children researching the news for science-related events and reporting back to the class.

Suitable for

KS1
KS2

Aims

- To use character, action and narrative to convey story, themes, emotions and ideas in plays they devise and script.
- To choose form and content to suit a particular purpose.
- To use and adapt the features of a form of writing.
- To review own work and the work of others and describe its significance and its limitations.
- To use writing to help thinking, investigating, organising and learning.

Organisation

- This is suitable for small groups of two to four

Resources

- Access to the internet

What to do

- Share some interesting science stories from the news.
- Children take it in turns to research an interesting science-related news story and then share this with the rest of the class. This can be done independently or in small groups. A presentation should be about five minutes long, with questions from the audience at the end.

- Sources to access include www.sciencenewsforkids.org, a dedicated science news website for children aged 9–14, BBC children's newsround pages at http://news.bbc.co.uk/cbbcnews, and newspapers, magazines, TV and radio. There are many interesting stories, especially animal stories (including animals that have never seen sunlight, pet blood banks, why NASA is sending worms into space, and why meerkats don't make good pets).

Variations

- The news item could be adapted into a story and told from the point of view of one of the people or animals involved.
- As a class, research a local science news item and video children relating the incident, facts, figures, opinions and points of view.

Have I got news for you

Have I got news for you involves completing headlines with a science-related theme and inventing new headlines using pictures from news.

Suitable for

KS1
KS2

Aims

- To use character, action and narrative to convey story, themes, emotions and ideas in plays they devise and script.
- To choose form and content to suit a particular purpose.
- To use and adapt the features of a form of writing.
- To review own work and the work of others and describe its significance and its limitations.
- To use writing to help thinking, investigating, organising and learning.

Organisation

- This is suitable for small groups of two to four

Resources

- Access to the internet

What to do

- Explain to children that a popular TV show includes a game where contestants have to guess the missing word from the covered-up section of a newspaper or magazine headline.
- Say that you have collected some of your own and the challenge is to fill in the blank or blanks with a word, phrase or rest of the sentence.

- You might decide to theme these. For example, the following headlines relate to smoking:

   Smoking gives you bad _____
   Smoking gives you bad breath

   Smoking makes your _____ and _____ stink!
   Smoking makes your hair and clothes stink!

   Once you start, _____ _____ ___ _____
   Once you start, it's hard to stop

   Children at risk from _____ _____
   Children at risk from passive smoking

   Higher risk of _____ _____ from smoking
   Higher risk of lung cancer from smoking

   Smoking ban _____ the _____
   Smoking ban clears the air

- Children can search internet science sites and science newspapers to create their own versions for other groups to try.

Variations

- Take a look at some pictures and photographs of animals or situations with a science slant and ask children to think of original and possibly humorous one-line captions or headlines to go with them. For example:

Wood you believe it? Habitats logging off by the minute.

There's no place like home.

Paws for thought: do alligators like stripes?
Tiger spots shopping trolley in river.
So that's what I look like.

- An extension or alternative to this idea involves children writing a newspaper headline and article in a tabloid style about an experiment they have just done. The article should be short and snappy with plenty to interest the reader. It can include quotes and images where appropriate. Finished newspaper articles can be displayed around the class.

Detectives

> Detectives gives life to science concepts by framing them as police investigations.

Suitable for

KS1
KS2

Aims

- To use character, action and narrative to convey story, themes, emotions and ideas in plays they devise and script.
- To choose form and content to suit a particular purpose.
- To use and adapt the features of a form of writing.
- To review own work and the work of others and describe its significance and its limitations.
- To use writing to help thinking, investigating, organising and learning.

Organisation

- This is suitable for small groups of two to four

Resources

- Copies of the story below

What to do

- Give children copies of the story below and read it together. For example:

My name's Detective Inspector Harry Bell, and I work for the City police department. When there's a problem, they ring for me. I've worked some pretty unusual cases in my time but the 'Shady' case kept everyone in the dark. Last year, I was called in to cast some light on the situation.

A guy by the name of Steve Shady walked into the station around midday to report a theft. He said that someone had stolen his shadow (well, most of it, he said) and he wanted us to help catch the light-fingered culprit. No one could work out why anyone would want to steal a shadow but, hey, the black market works in mysterious ways. Maybe shadows are worth a fortune these days.

This was a tough nut to crack but deceptively simple with the help of a bit of science training I'd done at school. None of my colleagues could see the light at the end of the tunnel but it eventually just came to me. There was no theft at all! Can you work out where Steve Shady's shadow disappeared to?

- Look at the text again and talk about the word play involved.
- Ask children to work in small groups to think of ideas about what happened to the shadow.
- Give children five minutes to frame an explanation for the detective.

Variation

- Children could write their own detective story to help with another science problem.

Science mnemonics

Mnemonics are great devices for helping to remember things. Science mnemonics encourages children to think creatively.

Suitable for

KS1
KS2

Aims

- To use character, action and narrative to convey story, themes, emotions and ideas in plays they devise and script.
- To choose form and content to suit a particular purpose.
- To use and adapt the features of a form of writing.
- To review own work and the work of others and describe its significance and its limitations.
- To use writing to help thinking, investigating, organising and learning.

Organisation

- This is suitable for small groups of two to four

Resources

- No special resources needed

What to do

- Explain to children that when we personalise learning we tend to remember things better, which is why mnemonics can work so well. Explain the word 'mnemonic' for anyone who does not know what one is.
- Common uses of mnemonics include remembering the colours of the rainbow or remembering the planets of our solar system. Show some examples of the latter by writing them on the whiteboard:

My Very Easy Method Just Speeds Up Naming Planets
My Very Energetic Mother Just Sent Us Nine Pizzas
My Very Eccentric Mother Just Served Us Nine Potatoes
My Very Early Morning Jam Sandwich Usually Nauseates People
My Very Exciting Magic Carpet Just Sailed Under Nina's Plimsol
Many Very Earnest Men Just Snubbed Unfortunate Ninth Planet
Most Volcanoes Erupt Mouldy Jam Sandwiches Under Normal
Pressure

- Tell children that Pluto is not classified as a planet any more so
  sentences don't have to include the letter P – but including it still
  allows for even better sentence building. Challenge them to think of
  their own versions to share with the rest of the class.

Variations

- Children could structure the mnemonic by drawing up a table like the
  one below:

Mercury	Many	My	My	My
Venus	Very	Vindictive	Very	Very
Earth	Elderly	Earwig	Elderly	Easy
Mars	Men	Might	Neighbour	Method
Jupiter	Just	Just	Just	Just
Saturn	Snooze	Sue	Sits	Seems
Uranus	Under	Us	Under	Useless
Neptune	Newspapers	Next	Nothing	Now

- Children could try to think of a mnemonic that also involves 'Milky Way
  Galaxy', such as My Very Educated Mother Just Served Us Nine Pizzas Made
  With Grapes. Mnemonics could also go from Neptune to Mercury.

Science idioms

There are lots of common everyday phrases that involve science words. Science idioms teaches children to decipher what they mean.

Suitable for

KS1
KS2

Aims

- To use character, action and narrative to convey story, themes, emotions and ideas in plays they devise and script.
- To choose form and content to suit a particular purpose.
- To use and adapt the features of a form of writing.
- To review own work and the work of others and describe its significance and its limitations.
- To use writing to help thinking, investigating, organising and learning.

Organisation

- This is suitable for small groups of two to four

Resources

- Science-inspired idioms list

What to do

- Explain to children that science has inspired some phrases that we use in everyday conversation but that their meaning may not be obvious.
- Write the idiom 'I'm always getting my wires crossed' on the whiteboard and ask children to tell you what they think it means. Have they ever heard it before? Have they used the phrase themselves?

- Now give children a copy of the list of science idioms below and see if they can work out what each might mean.

  I think I work best with Pippa because we seem to be on the same wavelength.

  I thought I'd be training hard until the competition. This was my Sputnik moment.

  I made a suggestion that went down like a lead balloon.

  It took a lot of elbow grease to get the shelter built but we did it.

- Look through the following idioms and split children into groups to solve a handful each:

Hit the airwaves	Walking on air
Light years ahead	No smoke without fire
It's not rocket science	Early bird catches the worm
Acid test	Eat like a horse
Add fuel to the fire	Many moons ago
All fingers and thumbs	Proud as a peacock
Left in the dark	

Variations

- Children can find a range of other idioms, such as idioms relating to parts of the human body, or create their own. Some examples for the human body are as follows:

As dry as a bone	Go belly up
A bone of contention	Bad taste in your mouth
Chilled to the bone	Elbow grease
Close to the bone	Knee-jerk reaction
A bundle of nerves	Heart of glass
At each other's throats	Eyes are bigger than your belly
At the top of your lungs	Get the cold shoulder
Bad blood	Have a chip on your shoulder
Blood is thicker than water	Get under my skin
Blood runs cold	A gut feeling
Blue blood	Joined at the hip

- Children could choose some idioms to use in sentences of their own, and act them out.

Acrostics

An acrostic is a poem or series of lines in which the first letters in each line form a name, motto or message when read in sequence. These can be used to great effect in a science context.

Suitable for

KS1
KS2

Aims

- To use character, action and narrative to convey story, themes, emotions and ideas in plays they devise and script.
- To choose form and content to suit a particular purpose.
- To use and adapt the features of a form of writing.
- To review own work and the work of others and describe its significance and its limitations.
- To use writing to help thinking, investigating, organising and learning.

Organisation

- This is suitable for small groups of two to four

Resources

- No special resources needed

What to do

- Explain to children that an acrostic poem is one where you choose a word or name and use each letter in the name as the beginning of a word or line that tells something about that person or topic.

- Show an example of a themed acrostic:

  Skeleton
  Cranium
  Incisor
  Enamel
  Nerve
  Calcium
  Elbow

- Now show children an acrostic poem with sentences.

  Sometimes when I go to the beach, I get sunburn.
  Unless I put on my sun cream of course.
  Noon is the time to stay indoors!

- See if children can invent acrostic poems for different types of cloud, either as one-word acrostics or as sentence poems.

Variation

- There are lots of poetry types to exploit beyond using acrostics. The poem below follows a recipe:

  Line 1 – the concept or process (one word)
  Line 2 – describe the meaning of the idea (two words)
  Line 3 – describe what the idea does (three words)
  Line 4 – say what the idea means to you (four words)
  Line 5 – an ending (one word)

  Dissolving
  Splitting apart
  Making smaller pieces
  Solid unites with liquid
  Physical

Concept sentences

Concept sentences asks children to make a sentence to show what they know about a topic. The sentence they create contains one or more key words.

Suitable for

KS1
KS2

Aims

- To use character, action and narrative to convey story, themes, emotions and ideas in plays they devise and script.
- To choose form and content to suit a particular purpose.
- To use and adapt the features of a form of writing.
- To review own work and the work of others and describe its significance and its limitations.
- To use writing to help thinking, investigating, organising and learning.

Organisation

- This is suitable for small groups of two to four

Resources

- Word mats, vocabulary lists and science dictionaries

What to do

- A list of key concepts is given to children, along with a list of linked relationship words to join them together with.
- Children can add to the list if they can think of any more words, or delete words if they do not understand them.
- Help children to start the activity by providing them with an example. On page 342 you will find a list of key words and link words. These

can be joined together by a relationship word or phrase – in this case, 'used to make'. This can be joined up with the key words 'plastic' and 'glass'. For example, plastic and glass are used to make doors'.

• Another example might be 'Many adhesives are toxic and should be avoided as they are bad for your health and the environment.' The number of words to include is up to you and should be tailored according to children's abilities.

Key words	Link words
wood is	a material
foam is	is
adhesives are	are
plastic is	light
rubber is	strong
steel is	hard
copper is	soft
wool is	flexible
silk is	stretchy
cotton is	rigid
nylon is	toxic
polyester is	absorbent
glass is	waterproof
metal is	heavy
paper is	light
brick is	made of
paint is	transparent
varnish is	opaque
lacquer is	properties
windows	used to make
buildings	can often be reused
furniture	because it is
floors	serious
cars	potential
clothing	environment
bags	health
cutlery	safety
plates and pens	
credit cards	
food packaging	
teabags	
coffee filters	
nappies	
napkins	

Variations

- Divide the class into groups and ask certain groups to focus on particular words.
- Display children's concept sentences for others to read and comment on.

A letter from an alien

A letter from an alien is an effective activity for getting children involved in some creative writing with a science twist.

Suitable for

KS1
KS2

Aims

- To use character, action and narrative to convey story, themes, emotions and ideas in plays they devise and script.
- To choose form and content to suit a particular purpose.
- To use and adapt the features of a form of writing.
- To review own work and the work of others and describe its significance and its limitations.
- To use writing to help thinking, investigating, organising and learning.

Organisation

- This is suitable for small groups of two to four

Resources

- Word mats, vocabulary lists and science dictionaries

What to do

- Show children the following letter you have received from an alien:

Dear Earth People,

We were passing your solar system the other day and we noticed that your planet seems to spin. We think you must all get very dizzy and things must move about a lot, get lost and fly off. Can you tell us how you cope?

From Jibnex and Jin-Jin, Planet Peace.

- Challenge the class to write a response using a scientific explanation.
- Children can work individually or create a response with a partner.
- When letters have been written, share responses and rate them as a class.

Variation

- There are many scientific concepts you can approach using this strategy. Here is another example:

    Dear Earth People,

    We have been looking at you with our telescope and we don't understand why one half of your planet seems to be in darkness and the other half in light. Does this mean that the plants on one side of the Earth never grow? We don't have this problem because we have four Suns and our planet is bathed in constant sunlight.

    From L56 and M9, Planet Radiance.

    Children can write their own alien letter and ask someone else in the class to reply to it. Display letters and replies in class.

Dear Doc

Dear Doc involves children writing to a fictitious doctor about a scientific problem they are experiencing. Children can write to the doctor or compose a reply as if they were the doctor.

Suitable for

KS1
KS2

Aims

- To use character, action and narrative to convey story, themes, emotions and ideas in plays they devise and script.
- To choose form and content to suit a particular purpose.
- To use and adapt the features of a form of writing.
- To review own work and the work of others and describe its significance and its limitations.
- To use writing to help thinking, investigating, organising and learning.

Organisation

- This is suitable for small groups of two to four

Resources

- Word mats, vocabulary lists and science dictionaries

What to do

- Show children the following letter and its reply:

Dear Doc Plantpot,

I was taking a walk around my garden the other day when quite out of the blue, a plant just exploded! I immediately ran inside to tell my family but they were glued to the TV as usual and not in the least bit interested. Tell me what happened here, Doc. I mean, was it something I said? Someone told me that talking to plants helps them to grow, not detonate! Should I play music? Should I apologise to the plant's family? Should I stay indoors and watch gardening programmes and let professionals take the risks? I didn't realise how dangerous gardening could be!

From Jane, aged 9.

Dr Plantpot replies:

This has clearly unsettled you, Jane, but hopefully my explanation will calm your nerves and nip this problem in the bud. Some plants naturally explode because it is a way of dispersing seeds. Several plants have fruits that burst quite violently. Most exploding fruits are capsules or pods. They lose water gradually and when they are dry they split apart, throwing out the seeds within, and they do this with some force. Some plants swell up with water. There's nothing wrong with talking to plants but touching them could be asking for trouble. Touch-me-not balsam fruits become so full with water that they explode at the slightest touch, hence their apt name!

- What do children think about the doctor's reply? Could they improve it?
- Now ask children to read the next letter and compose a reply as if they were the doctor.

Dear Doc Plantpot,

I just don't get it. I mean, I did something naughty, I know, but it seems to have backfired on me. Let me explain. I decided to plant a seed upside down so that the plant would grow into the soil and the roots would grow upwards. What a surprise I had when, after a few days, a stem appeared! How come when I planted the seed upside down?

From Navjot, aged 7.

Variation

- Children can write a letter, compose a reply *and* create a factsheet to go with the reply. An example is shown below:

Dear Dr Newton,

My dad has been trying to lose some weight (he's massive!). Mum read that there is a new health club opening on the Moon called Shedders. They say that anyone visiting the club is guaranteed to lose weight as soon as they set foot in the door. Dad's booked himself a place and is off next week! Will he lose weight that quickly or is he waisting/wasting his time?

From Nakita, aged 9 and a half.

Dr Newton says:

Nakita, the claims of the health club are absolutely right, but I suspect they are not telling your dad the whole story. You see, the Moon's pull is one-sixth that of the Earth. Let's imagine that your dad weighs 1,800 N on Earth; well, on the Moon he would weigh 300 N instantly. As soon as he came back down to Earth, he would weigh 1,800 N again! You'd better tell him before he makes a fool of himself. Why don't you give him a copy of my factsheet about weight loss? It's free and it might save him a few pounds! I'm sure your mum would like to read it too!

FACTSHEET: WEIGHING UP THE FACTS

Your weight will change depending on where you travel to in the solar system. If the force of gravity is different on another planet, then you could weigh less – but you could weigh more too! Your mass won't change wherever you take yourself. If you travelled to the Moon then your mass would be the same as it is at home here on Earth. That's because you contain the same amount of material. If it were possible to stand on the Sun (which I don't recommend) then you would weigh 28 times more than you do on Earth. Don't be fooled by the Solar System Travel Agents who sell weight-loss holidays to the Moon. You will lose weight but only while you are there! If you want to lose weight then the best thing to do is to exercise regularly and cut down on those calories!

Posters

> Posters challenges children to devise their own ways of communicating scientific ideas.

Suitable for

KS1
KS2

Aims

- To use character, action and narrative to convey story, themes, emotions and ideas in plays they devise and script.
- To choose form and content to suit a particular purpose.
- To use and adapt the features of a form of writing.
- To review own work and the work of others and describe its significance and its limitations.
- To use writing to help thinking, investigating, organising and learning.

Organisation

- This is suitable for small groups of two to four

Resources

- Word mats, vocabulary lists and science dictionaries
- Poster-making materials

What to do

- Challenge children to create an educational poster to show a particular process, to demonstrate a key concept, or to prepare an investigation: for example, the life cycle of a flowering plant, how to make a parachute, and so on.
- Choose two posters to focus on and ask the class to use two stars and a wish, 'What do we like? What suggestions could we make to help improve the posters?'

- Hold a poster conference: posters are left around the class on tables with a blank piece of paper next to each one.
- Groups then visit each poster and leave comments on the accompanying piece of paper. Authors then return to their poster and read the comments made.
- All groups can then respond to the comments made and defend their ideas if necessary. You could share posters with another class and hold a presentation.

Variations

- Hold a poster competition that the whole school can enter: for example, demonstrating how to wash your hands.
- Publish completed posters on the school website.

Build a dictionary

A great way to build vocabulary in science is to collect words and their definitions. This activity encourages children to make their own dictionary.

Suitable for

KS1
KS2

Aims

- To use character, action and narrative to convey story, themes, emotions and ideas in plays they devise and script.
- To choose form and content to suit a particular purpose.
- To use and adapt the features of a form of writing.
- To review own work and the work of others and describe its significance and its limitations.
- To use writing to help thinking, investigating, organising and learning.

Organisation

- This is suitable for small groups of two to four

Resources

- Access to the internet
- Word mats, vocabulary lists and science dictionaries

What to do

- There are lots of science dictionaries and their definitions can sometimes vary a great deal. Select a word or term and collect various definitions from dictionaries and the internet. See how much they differ.

- Challenge children to write their own straightforward versions of concepts. If possible, they should do this on a computer so that words can easily be added or edited and pictures can be copied and pasted from a variety of sources.
- Encourage children to think of what else they could put in their dictionaries that is not contained in others. Examples could include biographies of famous scientists, scientific words that have a non-scientific meaning, etc.

Variations

- Divide up the class into small groups and assign a letter to each. Tell children that it is their job to produce some helpful dictionary notes for a revision guide. They should summarise the key points using only headings and notes in a clear and engaging way. Encourage the use of illustrations (drawings, clip art, graphs, tables and diagrams) to make their pages attention-grabbing. Pool each group's pages and photocopy them to form a revision dictionary booklet on the topic. Each child receives a copy of the finished booklet.

Storyboard sequences

A storyboard is a sequence of pictures deliberately arranged to represent the events of a process, telling a story step by step. In this activity children use the storyboard sequence to explain a science process.

Suitable for

KS1
KS2

Aims

- To use character, action and narrative to convey story, themes, emotions and ideas in plays they devise and script.
- To choose form and content to suit a particular purpose.
- To use and adapt the features of a form of writing.
- To review own work and the work of others and describe its significance and its limitations.
- To use writing to help thinking, investigating, organising and learning.

Organisation

- This is suitable for small groups of two to four

Resources

- Word mats, vocabulary lists and science dictionaries
- Selection of images

What to do

- Explain to children that science processes can all be described as a sequence of events which happen over time and that these can be shown as a series of stages like a storyboard.

- For example, you could demonstrate the process of dissolving by taking some close-up photographs of the dissolving process. These can be printed off for children to sequence and explain.
- Another way of doing this is to present children with a grid like the one below and ask them to complete it showing how to make a perfect cup of tea. Alternatively, you could present six pictures or photos which show the six stages for children to turn into a flowchart.

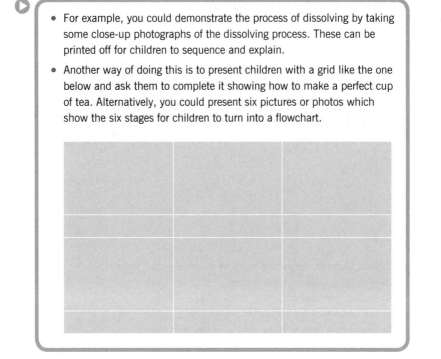

Variations

- Pupils could be encouraged to write their own instructions for other activities, such as how to make a pizza, how to clean your teeth, etc. Alternatively, show a storyboard in pictures for how to wash your hands or clean your teeth.
- Play a 'human flow chart' or storyboard game with children holding pictures of different stages in the process in the right order.

Science talk

Science talk challenges children to consider why it is important to use science-specific words in their writing and explanations.

Suitable for

KS1
KS2

Aims

- To use character, action and narrative to convey story, themes, emotions and ideas in plays they devise and script.
- To choose form and content to suit a particular purpose.
- To use and adapt the features of a form of writing.
- To review own work and the work of others and describe its significance and its limitations.
- To use writing to help thinking, investigating, organising and learning.

Organisation

- This is suitable for small groups of two to four

Resources

- Word mats, vocabulary lists and science dictionaries

What to do

- Tell children that when scientists do their work, they have a particular way of talking that helps them explain science ideas. Explain that scientists often use words that are similar, but not identical, to words one might use in another situation.
- Using one word as an example, explain or demonstrate how a science word can have a comparable everyday word (for example, 'observe', 'look').

- Highlight the differences in meaning between the science word and the everyday word.

- Make a class chart with two columns – one labelled 'Science word' and the other labelled 'Everyday word'.

- On the chart, record the everyday words that you read from a piece of text and see if children can translate them into a science word. Here are some examples to get you started:

Everyday word	Science word
home	habitat
soak up	absorb
top	surface
flop	wilt

Variations

- Children could be asked to use the everyday and science words in a variety of sentences.

- Read out the completed list of everyday words and ask children to think of the science words used instead.

Balloon debates

Balloon debates involves children deciding to eject someone from a balloon that is losing height. This can be used to discuss the contributions of famous scientists.

Suitable for

KS1
KS2

Aims

- To use character, action and narrative to convey story, themes, emotions and ideas in plays they devise and script.
- To choose form and content to suit a particular purpose.
- To use and adapt the features of a form of writing.
- To review own work and the work of others and describe its significance and its limitations.
- To use writing to help thinking, investigating, organising and learning.

Organisation

- This is suitable for small groups of two to four

Resources

- Word mats, vocabulary lists and science dictionaries

What to do

- Explain to children that four scientists are inside the basket of a hot air balloon which is losing height. To stay in the air, one of the scientists must leave the balloon.

- In groups of three or four, children discuss which scientist should be evicted from the balloon and then all ideas are shared. Possible scientists include:

  Michael Faraday
  Edward Jenner
  Isaac Newton
  Louis Pasteur
  Francis Crick
  Maurice Wilkins
  James D. Watson

Variations

- You could also hold a balloon debate as an odd one out activity and use concepts or words inside the balloon basket. Ask children to think of a reason why one should be asked to leave. For example, which one should go from this list?

  bone
  fizzy cola
  paper
  metal

- Another way to do this exercise is to look at healthy eating. For example, four friends take a ride in a hot air balloon. Unfortunately the balloon has a slow leak. The only way to keep the balloon airborne and prevent it from crashing is to throw things out. The friends all think about what they can do and start looking at their packed lunches. They decide the healthiest packed lunches can stay in the basket but one will have to go. Which lunch do children think the friends should get rid of?

  Wholemeal cheese salad sandwich, crisps, chocolate biscuit, blackcurrant juice drink
  Wholemeal egg mayonnaise sandwich, crisps, apple, yoghurt, orange drink
  Salad with grated cheese, crusty bread roll, Satsuma, fresh fruit salad, orange juice
  Cheese pasty, crisps, slice of cake, orange, lemonade

- Children can invent another 'food in a basket' problem using a different collection of meal options.

On the line

On the line challenges children to write an imaginary conversation between a customer and a shopkeeper in a science shop.

Suitable for

KS1
KS2

Aims

- To use character, action and narrative to convey story, themes, emotions and ideas in plays they devise and script.
- To choose form and content to suit a particular purpose.
- To use and adapt the features of a form of writing.
- To review own work and the work of others and describe its significance and its limitations.
- To use writing to help thinking, investigating, organising and learning.

Organisation

- This is suitable as a whole-class activity

Resources

- Word mats, vocabulary lists and science dictionaries

What to do

- Explain to children that they are going to listen to a conversation between a shopkeeper and a customer about a piece of scientific equipment or an idea.
- Read out the following script:

Phone rings:

Shopkeeper: Good morning, Science Shop, Matt speaking, how may I help?

Customer: Well, I've got a pretend skeleton I use in class to help teach children all about the bones, and one of the bones is broken. I dropped it carrying it from the resources cupboard.

Shopkeeper: I'm sure we can help. What's the bone called?

Customer: It's embarrassing but I can't remember the name of it.

Shopkeeper: Can you describe it to me please, sir?

Customer: Yes, it's the long bone in your leg that connects to the pelvis.

Shopkeeper: Ah, you mean the femur.

Customer: That's it! How silly of me, the femur, yes!

Shopkeeper: I'll just check the computer to see if we have any left, sir.

Customer: No, it's right I'm after, not left.

Shopkeeper: I didn't mean that, sir ... Never mind, yes, we have six right femurs left in stock, two human, three giraffe and one Jack Russell. It is a human femur you're after, isn't it?

Customer: Yes, human, yes. A right femur please.

Shopkeeper: Excellent, we are offering a two for one deal on human femurs until the end of the week if that's any interest to you sir, priced at £49.95?

Customer: Okay, I'll take them.

Shopkeeper: If I could just take your card number then please, sir ...

- In this example, the telephone conversation could be paused at the key moment before the bone is revealed. The rest of the class can write down what they think the bone is.

- The shopkeeper could also ask for help from the rest of the class by asking the 'shop manager' for assistance.

Variations

- This activity can be used in a variety of topics across the science curriculum.
- Challenge children to write their own telephone conversations and then act them out.

Recipe science

Recipe science engages children in a piece of creative writing in which they invent a recipe for making something or doing something.

Suitable for

KS1
KS2

Aims

- To use character, action and narrative to convey story, themes, emotions and ideas in plays they devise and script.
- To choose form and content to suit a particular purpose.
- To use and adapt the features of a form of writing.
- To review own work and the work of others and describe its significance and its limitations.
- To use writing to help thinking, investigating, organising and learning.

Organisation

- This is suitable for small groups of two to four

Resources

- Word mats, vocabulary lists and science dictionaries
- Selection of recipes from cookbooks

What to do

- Together look at some real recipes from cookbooks and discuss the list of ingredients and the language of instructions. Show children a couple of samples of scientific recipes, and discuss what elements they share with real recipes.

- Challenge children to write their own recipes around a concept, procedure or investigation. This can be serious or not so serious. Use the verbs below to help with the instructions if needed:

  > add, bake, barbeque, beat, blend, boil, braise, bread, broil, brown, chill, chop, coat, combine, cook, cover, deep-fry, dice, drain, fold in, freeze, fry, grate, grease, grill, grind, knead, marinate, mash, measure, melt, mince, mix, parboil, peel, poach, pour, puree, refrigerate, roast, sauté, scald, season, sift, simmer, slice, soak, spread, sprinkle, stew, stir, stir-fry, toast, toss, turn, whip.

Recipe for building a volcano

Ingredients:
- Pop bottle
- 60 ml water
- 15 ml of baking soda
- 60 ml vinegar
- Square of tissue paper
- Few drops of red food colouring
- Few drops of washing-up liquid
- Box to build model in
- Model trees, etc., for the surroundings

Instructions:
- First put 60 ml of water and a few drops of washing-up liquid into a pop bottle.
- Then add some food colouring and 60 ml of vinegar.
- Next, wrap 15 ml of baking soda in some tissue paper and twist the ends to make a little packet.
- When you are ready to make an eruption, drop the packet of baking soda into the bottle.
- You will see that the acid of the vinegar and the baking soda combine to make a lovely foam which froths and erupts. Enjoy.

Recipe for cleaning your teeth

Ingredients:

- Fluoride toothpaste
- Small-headed, soft-bristled toothbrush
- Some music of your own choice ($2\frac{1}{2}$ minutes)
- Egg timer or stopwatch

Instructions:

- First, press play on your MP3 and set your timer for 150 seconds.
- Next simply squeeze a pea-sized dab of paste on the top half of your brush.
- Then place your toothbrush at a 45-degree angle against your gums and gently move it in a circular motion.
- Hum along to your music and keep gently brushing.
- Gently brush the outside tooth surfaces of 2–3 teeth using a backwards and forwards movement.
- Move the brush to the next group of 2–3 teeth and do it again.
- Add more toothpaste if you wish.
- Brush your tongue from back to front to get off bacteria that will make your breath smell.
- When the timer rings have a good spit and rinse.
- Finish off with a good floss.
- Repeat at least twice a day.

Variations

- Ideas for recipes include instructions for helping a plant to grow, what you need for a successful habitat, things for a working circuit, etc.
- If you get enough recipes, you could publish a classroom cookbook.

Useful websites

The web is an almost infinite resource for accessing resources and help. Below are some websites that you may find useful. I have not listed many here because I think you will find that one good link leads to another and the websites here all connect to recommended sites worthy of your time.

The first port of call for all things science, the ASE website contains a wealth of information to help you teach science: **www.ase.org.uk**

Access a pile of resources for the Science QCA Scheme of Work from: **www. thegrid.org.uk/learning/science/ks1-2/resources/index.shtml**

Local authority websites can be a real hit and miss. The most worth looking at are:
www.sheffield.gov.uk/education/information-for-schools/good-practice/ curriculum/science/primary
www.eduwight.iow.gov.uk/curriculum/core/science/keystage2/SUBJECT.asp
www.lgfl.net/lgfl/leas/haringey/homepage/ (click on 'KS2 Science'.)

For ICT links go to the following address and type 'science' in the search box: **www.kented.org.uk/ngfl/**

Best school websites:
www.woodlands-junior.kent.sch.uk/revision/Science/
http://durham.schooljotter.com/coxhoe/Curriculum+Links

References and bibliography

Alexander, R. (2004) *Towards Dialogic Teaching*. York: Dialogos.

Black, P. and Wiliam, D. (1998) *Inside the Black Box*. London: King's College.

Black, P., Harrison, C. Lee, C., Marshal, B. and Wiliam, D. (2003) *Assessment for Learning*. Buckingham: Open University Press.

Bloom, J. (2006) *Creating a Classroom Community of Young Scientists*. New York: Routledge.

Farrow, S. (2006) *The Really Useful Science Book*. Abingdon: Routledge.

Garnett, S. (2002) *Accelerated Learning in the Literacy Hour Year 4*. London: Hopscotch Educational Publishing.

Harlen, W. (2001) *The Teaching of Science in Primary Schools*. London: David Fulton.

Herr, N. (2008) *The Sourcebook for Teaching Science*. San Francisco: Jossey-Bass.

Naylor, S. and Keogh, B. (2000) *Concept Cartoons in Science Education*. Sandbach: Millgate House.

Naylor, S., Keogh, B. and Goldsworthy, A. (2004) *Active Assessment in Science*. Sandbach: Millgate House.

'Warning'
by Jenny Joseph

When I am an old woman I shall wear purple
With a red hat which doesn't go, and doesn't suit me.
And I shall spend my pension on brandy and summer gloves
And satin sandals, and say we've no money for butter.
I shall sit down on the pavement when I'm tired
And gobble up samples in shops and press alarm bells
And run my stick along the public railings
And make up for the sobriety of my youth.
And shall go out in my slippers in the rain
And pick the flowers in other people's gardens
And learn to spit.

You can wear terrible shirts and grow more fat
And eat three pounds of sausages at a go
Or only bread and pickle for a week
And hoard pens and pencils and beermats and things in boxes.

But now we must have clothes that keep us dry
And pay our rent and not swear in the street
And set a good example for the children.
We must have friends to dinner and read the papers.

But maybe I ought to practise a little now?
So people who know me are not too shocked and surprised
When suddenly I am old, and start to wear purple.